C000184234

How To Love Bru- tal- ism

How To Love Bru- tal- ism

JOHN GRINDROD

BATSFORD

Contents

The Death and Life of Brutalism

Brutalism died on 3 March 1982. The Barbican Centre, part of an epic scheme of London Blitz rebuilding in the making since 1959, was opened by Queen Elizabeth, who said 'What has been created here must be one of the wonders of the modern world.' New commissions for brutalist buildings had been dwindling since the early 1970s, and a few more completions would straggle on until the mid-1980s in Montenegro, Lithuania and Crimea. After that, nothing. The whole architectural movement over, just 35 years since it had begun.

But that wouldn't be the end of the story. In fact, for many of us, encountering, inhabiting and admiring these strange and sometimes shocking buildings, it was just beginning. Because one of the most fascinating aspects of brutalism – that uncompromising, dramatic, wilful architectural style of rough concrete and asymmetrical awkwardness – is that despite repeated attacks from the media, developers, even the Queen's son Charles, loving brutalism has emerged as one of the most unexpected fetishes of the 21st century.

It's strange, the places you are drawn to. My list of favourites includes a mess of modern relics: glass towers and streets in the sky; moderne villas and concrete cathedrals. I am charmed by the lost townscape of London's Festival of Britain and its rugged South Bank successors. For Cold War cool, it is hard to beat Berlin's Fernsehturm television tower or the heroic United Nations Building in New York. The improbability of the nine connected spheres of the Atomium in Brussels and the 'stacked dishes' of the Sydney Opera House leaves me giddy. Such buildings are the products of many different schools of modernism, encompassing heroic and humanist; Scandinavian and East Coast; hi-tech and primitive. I'm beguiled by the lot. Yet one style has grown to dominate all others. For most of us, brutalism *is* modernism.

Marina City, Chicago, USA.

Architect: Bertrand Goldberg.

If brutalism has a problem, it is that for years we have been told that it cannot – no, *must not* – be appreciated. This view sees the buildings as ugly brutes that squat on our town centres and destroy the historic fabric of our cities. They are seen as soulless, sordid and beneath consideration, and best ignored. Those of us who have refused to turn our backs on it have had to learn a whole new way of appreciating it. I think it is no coincidence that brutalism's resurgence has coincided with the emergence of both the smartphone camera (the shy brutalist's enabler) and social media (providing motivation to take more photos). Together, they have broken a taboo around appreciating and photographing raw concrete buildings – secretly at first, and now ever more openly. Back in the day, you'd have had to lug round a bulky 35mm camera with an assortment of lenses, announcing your intention to record a building to all and sundry. Then suddenly pictures could be taken furtively, quickly and without anyone noticing. Rather than unavoidably parading your interest, you could instead draw it to the attention of likeminded 'brutalistas' across the globe, aided by the magic of social media subject hashtags and geolocation. Of course, we're now beyond that furtive era, and by the end of this book I expect you to be waggling your selfie stick around by your local bit of rough concrete and posting the resulting moody snaps on Instagram, Twitter and Tumblr. Oh, I see that you already are.

The evolution of brutalism is in some ways like that of the dinosaurs. Let's break it into three chunks, the brutalist versions of the Triassic, Jurassic and Cretaceous periods. In the brutalist 'Triassic' (pre-1950s), early forms emerged alongside other modernist styles, just as dinosaurs and reptiles grew and evolved together. Then in the brutalist 'Jurassic' of the 1960s everything became almost incomprehensibly massive. Looking at the size of brutalist buildings of this period, we can't quite believe how they came about. Then, by the 1970s, some most extraordinary manifestations occurred. This is the late flowering of 'Cretaceous' brutalism. Just as the dinosaurs evolved to coexist with more nimble mammals, so brutalist buildings mingled with new hi-tech and postmodern creatures. An asteroid obliterated the dinosaurs, and the evolution of brutalism came to an abrupt end with its own cataclysmic event: the global financial crisis of the 1970s that hit and wiped out future brutalist schemes. Today, the landscape is forever altered. The dinosaurs may have gone but the bones of the buildings remain to tell their story.

To some, the continuing existence of brutalist buildings is as challenging as the existence of dinosaur fossils to a creationist. Built from grit and sand and stone, rocks that have been crushed to minute fragments and have outlasted millennia, these buildings might seem beyond our opinions. Brutalist hulks, with their concrete walls, dark windows and rain-stained balconies, stare down uncomprehendingly at our attempts to project love and hate on them.

But without love, buildings decay and fall down. People cared to construct them, and they must care – love – to maintain them too if the structures are to remain part of our landscape. Vandalism and graffiti can ruin them. Buildings suffer under the onslaught of snowdrifts and leaves, wind and rain, and can be fatally damaged or even fall down. Human intervention is necessary to keep them standing and to maintain their façades and defences, so that they might continue to thrive.

With brutalism there are no easy fixes. Despite the awkward asymmetry and sheer sculptural weirdness, these structures only remain standing through continued love and admiration. They might look like the toughest buildings on the block, but these are delicate blooms. With most being bespoke rather than off-the-peg creations, maintenance is an issue. No two buildings have stairs, windows, walls or roofs configured in quite the same way. People often think of brutalism as an inexpensive sort of architecture but, as Dolly Parton once said, 'It costs a lot of money to look this cheap.'

In this book I aim to share my fascination for this extraordinary branch of architecture. I will take you through the different elements that make brutalism so special: its history and ideals, design and construction; the culture that surrounds it and its global impact; its brief flowering, sudden death and strange afterlife. We will travel back to its origins, meet the big names that brought it to life, rediscover some lost gems and explore brutalism's place in art, culture and history. Each of the stories and buildings along the way will tell us something about what makes this form of raw concrete building so worthy of attention. There will be tales of great creativity or domestic harmony, and others that are darker, exploring brutalism's flaws and the violence and destruction meted out by its critics.

For all its monolithic power, brutalism has never seemed more fragile or endangered. By learning to appreciate these buildings we can help preserve the riches of this strange and beguiling style. In this book I've tried to consider social history alongside art, architecture and design, to give some context to the work of the people who created brutalism. I'm aided in this by the enviable skills of The Brutal Artist whose beautifully detailed online illustration project has inspired many people's love of architecture. Still, I can't help thinking that if you need a book called *How to Love Brutalism*, then perhaps brutalism is not for you.

Paul Klee once famously remarked that 'drawing is taking a line for a walk.' Brutalism, it seems to me, is taking a line for a drive in a fast car, a subtitled film and a jazz cigarette. So get comfortable, fasten your seat belt and prepare yourself for a bumpy ride.

1.

<u>How</u>

<u>to</u>

<u>Hate</u>

<u>Brutalism</u>

and Other Opinions

Most of my friends and family don't like brutalism. I sometimes wonder what they must think when a photo of yet another concrete edifice appears on my Facebook page, or hear my tales of exploring behind the scenes at the National Theatre. Yes, that sounds really *interesting*, John. Not that I fall instantly in love with every grey, rain-stained hulk I see. The first time I heard 'Kiss' by Prince I doubled over laughing at his squeaky voice, the barely there instrumentation and the absurdly forward lyrics. But by the third time, I was convinced it was the greatest song I'd ever heard. For me, learning to love buildings often follows a similar pattern. Some are immediately charming and loveable. With others it sometimes takes me a couple of goes to 'get' it. And they are often the ones I end up loving the most.

There are people who throw out the phrase 'monstrous carbuncle' in relation to modern architecture as readily as Harry Potter would throw a spell. For them exposed, unadorned concrete seems a threat. Perhaps they think their boldly expressed dismay can magically transform blocks of flats or city centres into half-timbered thatched cottages or picturesque villages. Certainly there have been stylistic movements – Neo-Vernacular or New Classicism, for example – that are eager to cosy up to these more conservative contemporary attitudes.

Opponents of brutalism often seem to think that the people who like it are kidding themselves. They think it's intellectual posturing, a game played at the expense of the people who actually have to use these buildings every day. I am sure there are a few brutalistas to whom this applies, just as there are arch-ironists trumpeting everything from Baroque to mock Tudor. Accusations of elitism, what you might call let-them-eat-cakeism, hang over much discussion of modern architecture. They conjure up damaging images of thoughtless dilettantes condemning the poor and unfortunate to live in modernist housing estates, riddled with 'concrete cancer' and crime, places they wouldn't themselves dream of living in. Yet that doesn't explain why there are people queuing up to grab refurbished apartments in raw concrete masterpieces, such as London's Balfron Tower or Keeling House. Even if there are people who evidently like the buildings, this in turn throws up disturbing visions, of class cleansing and the privatization of council housing. Behind both scenarios, intellectual elitists or incoming apartment-dwellers, lie the real lives of those who have lived in brutalist flats since they were built. Their voices are usually ignored and selectively edited out of histories of the era. It is undeniable that many thousands of people were delighted to leave overcrowded, insanitary Industrial Revolution slums, and loved their new brutalist homes.

In the wake of the terrible Grenfell Tower fire of 2017, the reality of modern life in what remains of post-war social housing in Britain has been exposed. There are arms length management bodies, complex contracts for maintenance and refurbishment and decisions made over the wishes of the residents. They have combined to make many in social housing feel as powerless and exploited as the inhabitants of the 19th century-slums these buildings had been constructed to replace. These are not the fault of the buildings, but this political and market-led undermining of mass housing affects the lives of millions.

There have long been political reasons to undermine brutalism. These go back to the 1970s, and to the rise of free market economics that sought to sweep aside the post-war welfare states across Europe. Brutalism was one of the modern forms of architecture that came to be associated with the rise of council housing after World War II, and so it came under decades of sustained ideological attack by free marketeers in both government and the media. We are still seeing the results of this now, with council houses sold off in Britain and the remaining defunded social housing blocks blighted by maintenance and social problems, dismissed as a failure and demolished to make way for expensive private housing. The Grenfell Tower fire has to be seen against a political backdrop where regulations that might have helped save the lives of its overwhelmingly working-class tenants have been stifled. Criticism of brutalism is often tinged with class hatred, a desire for gentrification and a 'not in my back yard' wish for these easy symbols of poverty or immigration to be swept away.

The more superficial criticism is that modern architecture is ugly. Pick your brutalist insult: drab grey shitholes, monstrous carbuncles, depressing to look at, grim and joyless, a festival of monotony, a concrete jungle. Such views seem prevalent in local authorities and management boards, often keen to defund modern buildings so as to hasten their failure and collapse. Perhaps they have an eye to replacing them with the kind of red brick invisibles or glass box unknowables that developers favour today.

The material, concrete, is the reason most people give for dismissing brutalist buildings. Let's not mention that concrete appears in many of the most picturesque places in Britain – forming the piers and sea defences along our coast, or the steps through steep terrain – and is as ancient as the Romans. Perhaps behind this, these critics don't hate concrete so much as they hate cities. While fine in a wild landscape, seen in a city this oddly primitive material created from much older particles is dismissed as brash and aggressively modern. Those of us that live in cities appreciate the joy of their diversity – of the people, the districts and the buildings themselves. As time passes, brutalism becomes integrated as part of our historic fabric. Like the dormant volcanoes that have created the dramatic landscape of Edinburgh, say, it is no longer a threat. The fear, however, is that brutalism is going extinct.

2.

Concrete Beginnings

A Rough Time with Le Corbusier

You might have thought the first building to have the word 'brutalist' attached to it would have been a modest affair. A town house or a small villa, perhaps, built out of the way as a quiet experiment that would lead to bigger things. Instead, the first bit of overt brutalism was 12 storeys high, contained 337 apartments, a hotel, shops, a restaurant, a medical clinic, laundry, kindergarten and a gym – with a running track on the roof. This was Le Corbusier's housing unit, or Unité d'Habitation. It was not so much a block of flats as a whole vertical city.

For Le Corbusier (the pseudonym of Swiss-born Charles-Édouard Jeanneret), the Unité's brutality was the least of its attributes. He'd designed the structure around an idealized human form that he called the *Modulor*. The resulting semi-abstract figure might also have been his idea of the perfect resident: silent, decorative and, most importantly, created by him. The block itself was an experiment in living as a revolt against sprawling suburbanization. It was to operate as a machine, providing everything the inhabitants needed. These ideals went back to the 1920s, when Le Corbusier first became obsessed with a vision: cities constructed entirely of towers in parkland. This he explored in his 1925 Plan Voisin, imagining the demolition of a large area of Paris and its replacement with 60-storey towers surrounded by low-rise flats and green. The Unité d'Habitation, built 20 years later, showed he had lost none of his desire to shock.

Le Corbusier had adopted his pseudonym at the age of 33, when he became a journalist. His first major book, *Towards an Architecture*, was published in 1923 and was wide-ranging and confrontational. He gave readers a choice – *architecture or revolution?* – and contributed one of the most enduring tenets in modern architecture, the functionalist's creed – *a house is a machine for living in.* As one might have expected, the book included construction plans,

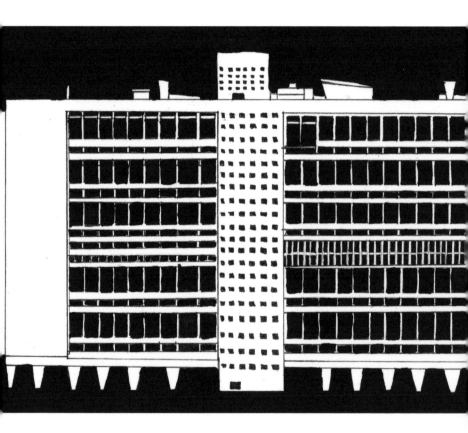

Unité D'Habitation, Marseille, France. Architect: Le Corbusier.

such as his 'Dom-Ino' frame – a two-storey house stripped back to show just the two floors, flat roof and supporting pillars between, somewhat resembling a coffee table. He was showing the potential of reinforced concrete, the free plan and free elevations it enabled in contrast to the heavy masonry and structure of traditional building techniques. With his prototype mass production house, 'Citrohan' he took lessons from the manufacture of cars and the design of aeroplanes and ocean liners. And he didn't stick to individual buildings – there were town planning ideas as well. The 'Ville Contemporaine' was based on earlier work by French architect Tony Garnier, where giant tower blocks sat at regular intervals in parks, gardens and playgrounds, away from a high-speed road network. Then there was a town raised up on pillars, where cars circulated on the 'service' level below and people roamed an artificial landscape on the first floor.

Towards an Architecture wasn't merely a book about design, it was a compelling series of statements linking ancient to modern, science to art and building to city. 'A man of today reading this book may have the impression of something akin to a nightmare' teased his translator, the English architect Frederick Etchells, like Alfred Hitchcock gleefully introducing a macabre story in his TV series. Etchells' introduction was instructive on how Le Corbusier's work was likely to be received in Britain: 'I have no doubt that some of the French work illustrated in these pages will appear unpleasing to many of us,' he remarks, emphasizing the gulf between Continental modernism and the conservative British architecture establishment of the day. The remark was prophetic when it came to Le Corbusier's later adoption of brutalism.

The 'brut' in 'brutalism' did not come from Le Corbusier, but rather from the material that he was using to construct his enormous housing unit: *raw* concrete, or *béton brut*. This sense of 'raw'-ness is lost in English, and instead a violent, thuggish, disturbing undertone predominates, with 'brutal' in mind – buildings that brutalize the inhabitants. Rather than being clad in a more 'respectable' material such as stone, Le Corbusier's Unité revelled in the imperfections of its uncovered raw concrete. It made for a confrontational statement in Marseilles, where it was constructed between 1947 and 1952. The concrete was left to set in wooden moulds or 'shutters', and it was these roughly constructed boxes that helped to create the counter-intuitively primitive finish of this resolutely modern structure. It was yet another example of the collision of ancient and modern in Le Corbusier's work: an immaculate grid created from the most impure and organic of materials.

Upon completion, the Unité became an instant hit with architects, who made pilgrimages to Marseilles from all over the world. The locals, meanwhile, were rather less impressed and called it La Maison du Fada – the madhouse. Regardless, it was the sheer audacity of Le Corbusier's vision that inspired his peers, and the boldness of his use of raw concrete fired their imaginations. Since the mid-19th century, architects had viewed it as the perfect plastic material, one that could be moulded into any shape. But architects had been nervous of using it extensively in domestic buildings. Now this new generation saw that it did not even need to be prettified for domestic use. Instead, concrete's rough stony texture was appealing in itself. The idea of being able to put up a massive structure without a steel frame was also attractive to cost-conscious architects, who were looking for practical solutions they could take home and introduce to austerity-pinched local authorities or private practice.

It is curious that it was the concrete from which the Unité is made, rather than its other innovations, that it would become best known for. While Le Corbusier's *Modulor* system was imitated by other architects, such as Ernő Goldfinger in his two famous London towers, Trellick and Balfron, it was largely dispensed with by others. The idea that one building could house so many different functions is common today, but is usually achieved with rather less panache or coherence. And despite a glut of smart gadgets, we are still some way from houses that provide for the inhabitant's every need.

Le Corbusier intended to see other iterations of his Unité built, and his desire was satisfied by a further series of commissions: in Nantes-Rezé (1955), Berlin (1957), Briery (1963) and Firminy (1965). The five Unités continue to inspire architects and residents today, their colourful balcony façades and rough concrete 'bottle rack' structure are an enduring symbol of modernity that helps place all future brutalism into historical context. Le Corbusier continued to push the primitive aspect of his muse, but it was this gloriously awkward behemoth that would come most to fascinate the architects who followed.

3.

Brutal Ethic or Aesthetic?

The Moral Case for Brutalism

Brutalism may have been created by Le Corbusier, but it was codified by critic Reyner Banham as 'New Brutalism' in a 1955 essay for *The Architectural Review*. So taken was Banham that he extended this magazine essay into a full-scale book, *The New Brutalism: Ethic or Aesthetic* (1966).

A lanky hipster with black-rimmed specs and a great bucketful of beard, Banham looked every bit the earnest and evangelical owner of a trendy microbrewery. What attracted him to brutalism was the earthy purity promised by this new style, one of many in the booming arts scene of the 1950s and early 60s. Brutalists rubbed alongside the 'angry young men' – and women – of post-war literature and drama; their social realist filmmaker cousins; the visual movements of outsider art and art brut; in music, the exponents of musique concrète, experimental jazz and new-fangled rock 'n' roll. With their energy, the uncompromising nature of their expression, their rebellion against cosy established norms and their bold representation of everyday life, these artists and thinkers shook up a world that was still emerging from shortages and the long shadow of war. Observing the rather eclectic grab of art and architecture that Banham used to illustrate his original magazine article, journalist Catherine Slessor recently joked on Twitter that it looked more like a deadline crisis than the birth of an architectural movement. 'My theory of Reyner Banham and the New Brutalism,' she wrote, 'Long lunch. Pub in the basement. Deadline looming. Random stuff in drawers. Wing it.'

The subtitle of *The New Brutalism: Ethic or Aesthetic* shows where the culture wars were at the time. Banham merrily slags off milder Scandinavian forms of modernism as mere superficial 'aesthetic' whereas 'gritty' brutalism is ruled by a solid philosophical 'ethic'. But, strangely, you could equally well reverse these. The humanism of the Scandinavian designers, providing for a welfare state age, points to an ethically driven architecture. Even the Scandinavians'

much-derided attempts at picturesque townscape and 'people's detailing' seems less of an aesthetic decision than one growing out of humanist notions of relating everything – be it tower blocks or schools – back to human scale. Meanwhile, rufty-tufty brutalism could be seen as a rather more aesthetic school, where sculptural qualities and an obsession with purity of form often dominate thoughts of mere function. Whatever the case, it's clear that in its various forms brutalism can be both ethic *and* aesthetic.

For me, the ethics of brutalism doesn't begin and end with the purity of the makers. Instead, like the new humanists, the ethical dimension of their work comes from their co-option into the housing and welfare state programmes of countries across Europe. Contemporary architects such as Rem Koolhaas, Daniel Liebskind and Zaha Hadid have produced designs as rebellious as any of the world's great post-war masterpieces, and as sculpturally dynamic. What they haven't done so much is design the essentials of modern life, as the brutalists did: social housing, hospitals, libraries and bus stations. More often, contemporary architects are drafted in to provide cities with new 'icons' – office towers, museums, galleries or luxury apartments. It is in its everyday application that brutalism finds both its soul and its ethical dimension. Over and above the abstract intention of the architects, much of their success came instead from the kind of work they were doing, and their astonishing responses to those commissions. They were designing, to borrow a current advertising slogan from Ikea, 'the wonderful everyday'.

This second wave of modernists rejected the soft-edged sell-out of their elders, and produced angry manifestos to justify why. Chief among them was an acerbic young British couple, Peter

Smithdon High School, Hunstanton, UK.
Architects: Alison and Peter Smithson.

and Alison Smithson. You can get a good idea of them from *The Smithsons on Housing*, a 1970 documentary in which they discussed the making of Robin Hood Gardens, their imposing housing estate in East London. Alison, with a shrill, cracked voice, and Peter, speaking in a paternalistic tone, stare down the uncomfortably close camera lens. She wears a homemade silver dress, he a silver tie; they are every inch the architects who fell to Earth. Their manifesto for the New Brutalism, some 15 years earlier, had been published alongside Banham's piece in a 1955 edition of *Architectural Design* magazine. 'The New Brutalism is the only possible development *for this moment* from the modern movement' they insisted. In the pure use of materials – concrete, glass, brick, steel – they saw a 'realisation of the affinity which can be established between buildings and man.' But it wasn't just about materials. The Smithsons were quick to make a link between this new sensation and the rise of pop art, at the same time disrespecting the more 'worthy' endeavour of the Arts and Crafts tradition: 'It has nothing to do with craft. We see architecture as the direct result of a way of life.' And, just as in pop art, this approach was a way of life brought about by modernity – convenience products, kitchen equipment, furniture, cars and sci-fi imagery.

Smithdon School, the Smithsons' debut, was to be Britain's first chunk of brutalism. Surprisingly, it took its reference not from Le Corbusier but from another titan of early modernism, Mies van der Rohe; in particular, from his cool, noirish engineering classrooms at the Illinois Institute of Technology. The Smithsons' riff on this design called for local yellow gault bricks, standard steel sections bought off the shelf, a Braithwaite water tower (of the sort used to refill steam engines on the railways) and lots of glass. Ever the educated historians, Peter and Alison claimed to be 'using the steel in the same way as medieval builders used wood.' Despite their disdain for arts and crafts, their vision would have more in common with the hand-tooled machismo of ancient construction techniques than it would with the Scandi-style prettification of the Festival of Britain, say, or a 1920s 'white box' building. In Hunstanton, the steel frame would be as visible as the wooden frame on a Tudor manor house.

The Smithsons would often talk about how their architecture was inspired by the ways in which people lived. Nigel Henderson's photos, of working-class kids playing on the streets outside their slum houses or the adults whose social lives also spilled onto the pavements, were often cited as a major factor in their thoughts. But in Hunstanton there was little evidence of this social concern being put into practise. They didn't visit the site or speak to educationalists before designing the school, and they weren't keen on the kids being photographed in it after it was finished. Ethic or aesthetic, then?

Critics were confused by what the Smithsons were up to. Nikolaus Pevsner thought the school entirely unbrutal: 'It is symmetrical, clean, precise – in short Mies van der Rohe and not Le Corbusier in origin.' It was typically perverse of the Smithsons to claim that brutalism owed more to Mies van der Rohe than it did to Le Corbusier, whom everyone else thought of as its spiritual godfather. In some ways it is as if the Smithsons set out to deliberately troll the modern establishment, by making sweeping statements that seemed to contradict the general direction of play. The divergence between the approaches of Le Corbusier and Mies went back decades. Back in 1932 the Museum of Modern Art in New York had held a provocative show called the International Exhibition of Modern Architecture. More than half of the exhibition was taken up with examples from Europe, with star pieces from Le Corbusier, Mies and Walter Gropius. The curators, Philip Johnson and Henry-Russell Hitchcock, coined the term International Style to describe the exhibits, and defined the concept with a number of underlying principles: architecture as volume, showing how the structural skeleton was supported by columns which added flexibility to the finished building; regularity, through a clear expression of the inner workings, repetition and the use of standardized elements; and an avoidance of applied decoration.

It was interesting that curators Hitchcock and Johnson avoided many of the other ingredients that the modernists were keen on, including the social, planning and functional concerns of Le Corbusier. Instead they focused on stylistic elements, such as regularity – bringing them more in line with Mies' philosophy. By reducing the International Style movement to these few design tics they separated the ideological from the formal, in the process stripping the movement of all but its most pragmatic and superficial motifs. It helps to explain why Reyner Banham was so focused on defining whether brutalism was an ethic or an aesthetic – he was working out in what ways it was different from the slick international fashion of the age. These were the kind of fiercely fought philosophical arguments that dominated modern architecture in the mid-20th century, and it was against this backdrop that forceful younger designers such as the Smithsons attempted to push modernism on. In many ways you can see the consequence of all of this antagonism in the work of this second generation of architects: they tackled their projects with an unapologetic boldness, in order to stake out the very frontiers of modernism as their domain, reacting against the cautious pragmatism of much private and public design.

For such a creative power couple, Peter and Alison Smithsons' practice would be sadly starved of major projects. Their Economist Plaza in London, unbrutally clad in Portland stone, was perhaps their most celebrated project, while ambitious designs for Coventry Cathedral, the Golden Lane estate in London and the Hauptstadt in Berlin all remained unbuilt. Still, they would eventually get the chance to design a housing estate in their favoured style.

Robin Hood Gardens (1968–72) in East London has been in the slow process of being demolished for what seems like the past ten years. Even when it was finished this rough concrete estate was a place out of time, designed around the 'streets in the sky' idea they had helped to pioneer two decades before. By the time the Smithsons got their chance to have a go they were one of its final exponents. Today, as the demolition crews and developers move in, Robin Hood Gardens has become a brutal full stop from the couple who kick-started the conversation in the first place.

We might love the buildings, but how to love the Smithsons? Well, despite their fearsome reputation, a good way to start would be reading the essay on Alison Smithson by Rachel Cooke in her book *Her Brilliant Career*, which shows a more human side to the architect. Here we see a woman breaking creative boundaries in the 1950s and 60s, pioneering a world-imitated architectural style, bringing up kids and writing the odd terrible novel in her spare time. Without the Smithsons' drive and commitment back in the 1950s it might be that brutalism would have remained a fringe attraction rather than become one of the central schools of architecture of the age – by anyone's reckoning, an impressive achievement.

4.

The Nitty-Gritty:

Griffy:

How Brutalism is Made

I t's all very well architects arguing over the finer points of philosophy, but brutalism is as much about the nitty-gritty of gravel and cement as it is about artistic expression. It was down to engineers and builders to interpret these highfalutin ideas and bring them into reality. Sometimes they would influence the architects so strongly, with all the new possibilities of construction available, that they would in turn act as both muse and creators in this relentless rush of innovation.

Initially the modernists' use of reinforced concrete was half-hearted compared to the swaggering feats of engineering going on at the same time. Ove Arup, the great 20th-century engineer, wrote in 1926 that 'the best architecture in reinforced concrete is generally that to be found among those big engineering structures' – by which he meant bridges, silos, hydraulic dams and the like. But it wasn't so great for creating places you could live in. Problems such as heat loss and noise penetration meant that this interwar concrete was a flawed material, used as it was very thinly for walls. But such was the speed at which the science of concrete engineering moved that within 15 years these issues had been largely addressed, if not entirely solved. Water penetration and staining remained hard problems to beat, and the addition of asbestos cement as insulation in some schemes has not left a happy legacy. Still, without constant advances in chemical science and construction techniques much of modern architecture would never have been possible.

Ove Arup was a trusted lieutenant to the new architecture establishment. He was just one of a great number of structural engineers who made the abstract dreams of modern architects a concrete reality (often literally). There was Owen Williams, who as well as being one of the foremost engineers of interwar modernism, worked on many of the great road schemes in Britain such as the Gravelly Hill interchange near Birmingham, better known as that dizzying landmark, Spaghetti Junction. The Smithsons relied on the practical nous of Ove Arup employee Ron Jenkins to realize their demanding Smithdon school design. And perhaps most crucially, the epic concrete dreams of Oscar Niemeyer at Brasília could not have come to pass without the extraordinary engineering genius of Joaquim Cardoso, a published poet, short-story writer and editor.

One of the most appealing aspects of brutalism is the coming together of the different skills of architect, engineer and builder to create something genuinely new. Not that everything always worked smoothly. Arup, for one, could be scathing about the designs he was presented with. But ever the problem-solver he would look to ways to improve them and turn them into reality. Writing in the January 1969 edition of *Structural Engineer* magazine, he described architects as 'prepared and indeed determined to design their buildings in reinforced concrete – a material that they knew next to nothing about – even if it meant using concrete to do things that could be done better and more cheaply in another material.' The architects' demands placed a heavy burden on the engineers, who, in a pre-computer age, had teams of people engaged for months to work out the complex calculations and formulas needed to ensure these new and challenging designs were structurally sound.

There is, of course, nothing innately modern about concrete, this Roman leftover rediscovered by the Victorians. As Adrian Forty writes so beautifully in his book, *Concrete and Culture*, it is a material that is equal parts chemistry and physics. The engineers deal with the physics, and the construction companies with the chemistry. An average batch of concrete might be made from one part Portland cement, two parts dry sand, three parts dry stone, and half a part of water. To strengthen it, steel reinforcing bars, or rebars, are laid in the formers and cooked into the concrete like a sixpence in a Christmas pudding. This extra ingredient, the reinforcing, was developed in the

19th century. It was followed in 1905 by the concrete mixer, which helped concrete on its way to become a truly mass-produced material.

Whether on site or in a factory, concrete components are created using formwork or shuttering. These are the jelly moulds: wooden boxes that get filled with poured concrete. The secrets of good shuttering are as complicated as those for good concrete. The trickiest hazard can be that the concrete leaks into the wooden formwork and so becomes impossible to separate from the mould once dry. Unlike wood or stone, concrete doesn't really have its own shape, and so instead takes on the ghost of whatever it's moulded in. We see these formwork phantoms in the finish of many modernist structures, inside and out. There's the intimate detail of wooden planks on the walls at the National Theatre in London, where the mix of aggregates (marine-dredged ballast, fine aggregate of Leighton Buzzard sand, two types of waterproof cement) was very carefully monitored to get that exact result. But these striations aren't always the desired effect. A rougher aggregate, using bigger pebbles, was used for Basil Spence's short-lived Glasgow landmark; the Queen Elizabeth Square flats, where evidence of the moulds was writ large rather than small. Meanwhile at the Barbican in London, the finish of the formwork was obliterated, as every granite-dust concrete surface was meticulously bush-hammered by hand to give it that distinctive rugged, rocky appearance. Extravagant experiments yielded other, yet more complex, results. Concrete fetishist Paul Rudolph favoured a technique called 'roping', which created channels to direct water downwards, leading the weathering to occur in the grooves rather than across all the surfaces.

Of course, not all brutalist buildings are overwhelmingly concrete. Take the sturdy Ham Common flats designed by James Stirling and James Gowan in South West London, at Langham House Close (1957–58). Here, the concrete frame is filled in by

reused yellow London stock brick, creating something that is at once locally familiar and startlingly new. The solid two- and three-storey flats run along a slender side road, their squat forms defined by the hefty concrete beams carrying the load of the structure. Greater London Council architect Kate McIntosh would take this approach much further, reacting against the harshness of what she saw as an overreliance on concrete for her masterpiece, Dawson's Heights (1964–72), in East Dulwich, London. The two main blocks of the estate exaggerate the hilltop on which they are built, creating a red brick and concrete crest, with balconies jutting out to create a fascinating irregular pattern across the surface of these great brutalist ziggurats. Like the Ham Common flats, they are a reminder of the variety of materials embraced by a style that is now remembered only for one.

Queen Elizabeth Square flats, Glasgow, UK.
Architect: Basil Spence.

5.

<u>Unbrutal</u>
<u>Truths:</u>

The Modernist Rivals
to Brutalism's Crown

I f you have ever posted in a brutalist architecture fan group online, you'll be aware of two tendencies. Firstly, there's the purist, who wants to purge the group of mention of any structure that falls outside of a rigid definition of the topic. And then there's the catholic, who wishes to claim all of the best bits of 20th-century design as brutal, regardless. Civil war generally ensues between these roundheads and cavaliers, and little is achieved. Yet outside of those closed communities, the way people generally bandy about the word brutalism you'd think it was a catch-all term for anything put up during the Cold War. Some people – say it softly – might even claim brutalism is just a school within the International Style, and a minor one at that. True, brutalism wasn't even the dominant type of architecture in the mid-to-late-20th century. Back in the 1920s and 30s European tastemakers had been entranced by 'weightless' white box modernism – villas, health centres and pavilions floating on slender columns – in designs heavily influenced by the gleaming ocean liners of the day. And by the 1950s – well, not much had changed. This fastidious – but no longer provocative – style was still much in evidence, in places such as the Festival Hall on London's South Bank – all long horizontal windows, white façades and pillars. And the International Style would go on to rival brutalism when it came to building the monumental, with town halls, office towers and even the UN Headquarters in New York encapsulating the formal grid and lighter-than-air theatrics of boxes on columns and podiums.

Across Scandinavia, the movement coalesced in a more unpretentious down-home style that became known as humanism. Here the detailing was charming, the lines clean and elegant, the forms often modest and functional. The most ubiquitous of these developments came from Sweden in the shape of the 'point block'. Born in the mid-1940s, the point block was a sort of high-rise in which the elevators and stairs made up a central spine around which

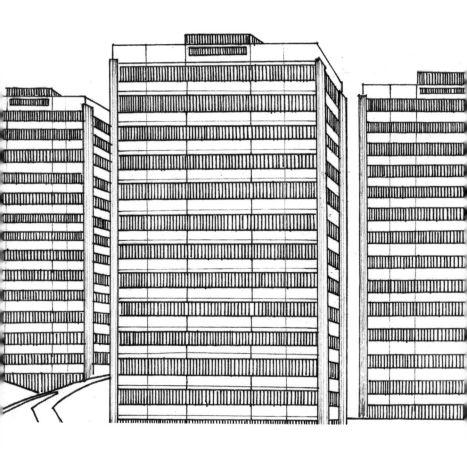

Castle Vale Estate, West Midlands, UK.

Building contractor: Bryant.

the flats clustered. Within 20 years this sort of tower was to become one of the most ubiquitous types of social housing around the world, whether in the projects of Pruitt-Igoe in St Louis, or the Ang Mo Kio (AMK) flats in Singapore. The original idea, of the tower being part of an estate of high-rise flats, low-rise blocks and houses, was meant to add variety and human scale into planning and design, a field that became known in Britain as 'townscape'. Scandinavian humanism and the cool lines of International Style chime most closely with our current obsession with vintage bric-a-brac and 'mid-century modernism' – the cute teak furniture, elegant blown glass, atomic-patterned fabrics and decorative ceramics so redolent of an optimistic, consumerist post-war age. Two of those point blocks in London – newly built Ronan Point, which partially collapsed in 1968 and newly refurbished Grenfell Tower, which burned in 2017 – now haunt all further discussion of them.

While the debate raged over style, philosophy and function, architects found themselves overtaken by events. A rather different player emerged in the 1940s that would end up responsible for the majority of mass housing projects around the world. This was system building, or construction via prefabricated flat-pack. The protagonists were engineers and construction companies, not architects. Sure, prefabrication had been tied up with modernism from the very beginning. Le Corbusier's obsession with machines for living in extended to the machines that might create them. Production lines, such as those manufacturing cars, ships or aeroplanes, were a major achievement of modernity, and designers were keen to take advantage of them. But in the end it wouldn't be the architects who broke through with production line buildings. Instead, it was a succession of construction companies, inventing prefabrication systems that they exported around the globe. France and Scandinavia led the way. Popularly used systems – Camus, Sectra and Tracoba – originated in France, while others – Skarne, Jespersen and Larsen-Nielsen (the system used to build Ronan Point) – came from Sweden and Denmark. Across the Communist bloc, a decree by Nikita Khruschev in 1957 led to an obsession with using a small number of systems to create blocks of flats of identical design stretching from Siberia to Poland.

These kits could be made in specialized factories, either on or off site, and the components bolted together by relatively unskilled labour, unlike the much slower processes of traditional construction techniques and exacting architect designs that required the services of skilled, experienced builders. The 'off the peg' prefabricated structures are the ones most commonly lumped in with brutalism, largely because most of the components were made from rough concrete. But on the whole, true brutalist edifices tended to be architect designed and use bespoke moulds and parts rather than the products of these mass-produced systems. Just because these are other types of modernism doesn't mean we have to dismiss or row about them, as the architects of the day undoubtedly did. But, equally, we don't have to love them either. These prefabricated systems were used to construct much of the fabric of our welfare states, which goes in their favour. But they were often hastily constructed and poorly assembled. I've written more extensively about the success or otherwise of these forms of architecture in my book *Concretopia* (2013).

International Style, humanist, prefabricated. Each approach has its merits, and I love many of the resulting buildings. Some brutalistas may sneer at the anguished post-war theatrics of Coventry Cathedral, where art and architecture entwine to produce a place of great spirituality and beauty. Meanwhile, the atomic age graphic devices of Mies van der Rohe make the city a cartoon. His steel and glass grids create a vista of two-dimensional planes among the three-dimensionality of all those 19th-century villas, terraces and skyscrapers. These lighter-than-air structures have none of the monumental heft of their raw concrete cousins. And don't forget that those system-built towers and estates were once the most go-ahead way of housing people in an era of tremendous shortages, and so have a moral dimension that makes them captivating, despite attempts to compromise them.

Appreciating post-war modernism in all of its hues helps contextualize brutalism, where the dramatic sculptural bluntness often sits in glaring contrast to the mildness, functionalism and streamlined cool of other styles. Yet we still see those decades-old arguments played out on message boards and Facebook groups, where the factions are often less flexible than the architects of the day, many of whom worked across two or more of these styles, sometimes simultaneously. In order to love brutalism, you should attempt to embrace these and other contemporaneous approaches too because, like all great architecture, it makes most sense when seen in context rather than isolation.

6.

Big.
Brutes:

Pioneers and their Peccadilloes

I f the inspiration behind brutalism came from Le Corbusier and
was codified by Peter and Alison Smithson, its practice came from
a mixture of big brutes – the great names of the modernist era –
along with some jobbing architects working for commercial and
local authority practices, who were aiming for something a bit special.
What, if anything, did they have in common? A desire for social
justice? A search for artistic purity? An ideology? A need for cold,
hard cash? Truth be told, their motivations were pretty varied, even if
their combined work coalesced into something rich and strange.

The greatest rival to Le Corbusier's crown as King Brutalist
might have been the Brazilian Oscar Niemeyer. His fondness for
fluid curves in concrete created a whole new language in modernism.
As a young man he had worked with Le Corbusier in Brazil. 'From
the outset,' remarked the old crow, 'Niemeyer knew how to give full
freedom to the discoveries of modern architecture.' Niemeyer's long
and productive life – he died aged 104 – also allowed him to take
on a lot of projects. His take on working with concrete was to push
the expressive and sculptural elements. Brasília, the new capital,
would become his most inspiring canvas, and on it he produced
masterpiece after masterpiece. National Congress Building, Supreme
Court, Presidential Palace, National Theatre, Cathedral of Brasília,
all products of his fertile, restless and sensuous imagination. 'My
work is not about "form follows function",' he proclaimed, 'but "form
follows beauty" or, even better, "form follows feminine".' As happy
designing schools as he was the cradle of government, Niemeyer saw
his architecture as something for everyone, not just an elite project for
the few, or as quick mass housing for the poor. Brazil's desire for rapid
transformation matched his progressive politics and his ambition – at
least until he, like the left-wing government that sponsored him and
Brasília, fell from favour in the 1960s.

Another of the early greats was Bauhaus student and, later, lecturer, the Hungarian Marcel Breuer, whose brutalism is crystalline and classically tinged. Initially he was known for startlingly robust furniture design, much of which remains popular today. But it was his fascination with reinforced concrete and the flexibility it offered that led him to create his most remarkable objects. And he broke the purists rules: sometimes his architecture was built from bespoke parts, but he also designed prefabricated kits to use across multiple projects. Much as his furniture had looked sturdy enough to be architecture, a great deal of his architecture would look like furniture scaled up to immense size. These buildings were the coffee tables, room dividers and sideboards of the gods. He worked in the International Style for the Unesco Headquarters in Paris (1952–58), with its giant three-spoked check-in desk. By contrast, the startlingly blocky Whitney Art Gallery in New York (1963–66) is like a gigantic safe, keeping all of the precious artworks locked away. There's even a single projecting window onto Madison Avenue that makes for a perfect combination dial. Then there were two masterpieces he created for IBM: a research centre on a rugged slope at La Gaude, France (1958–62) and another on the flat plain at Boca Raton, Florida (1968–74). Both are languid low-rise slabs suspended on tall Y-shaped columns that might be a couple of *chaise longues* for Godzilla. Breuer was 'A Good Thing': he was a progressive employer of women, had utopian ideas of creating a better world, and wasn't afraid to go against the prevailing voices of the day. No head stuffed with concrete here.

Working on an epic scale was the obsession of American architect Paul Rudolph, the wizard of rough concrete. He'd studied under Breuer and Walter Gropius, and found his skill lay not just in the creation of single buildings but also in the dramatic sweep of urban planning, for which he was much in demand. A fan of the megastructure, many of his schemes are insanely complex, combining numerous different uses into single entities. Rather more contained is his rugged Yale Art and Architecture Building (1958–64). What better way to introduce a generation of architects to his favoured style than to design a brutalist school for them? Here, as in many of his works, he favoured a heavy, butch aesthetic over the poised weightlessness of the International Style. This is what people regard as the 'massive' era of brutalism, where all forms were exaggerated, working that 'on steroids' look. The building was smothered in tons of hand-bashed ribbed concrete, a finish familiar to fans of London Zoo's Elephant House. This Rudolph speciality finish is everywhere, coating the colossal piers and pillars that form the structure, both inside and out. The heart of the building was an open atrium, with balconies allowing newcomers to look down on the older students at work, and at a colossal classical statue of Minerva. It's a view creating both a sense of hierarchy and bustling openness. Fire broke out and gutted the Yale building in the late 1960s. No culprit was ever found. For the students, who are often blamed for the blaze, the massive form with its rigid social hierarchy had characterized the patrician and repressive university administration in the days of the civil rights and anti-Vietnam struggles. Know your place, it seemed to say. Perhaps they had their own view on the building's place. Maybe it was a tragic accident, or some secret fault lay at its heart, waiting to erupt. Rudolph's career is a curious one. Despite all his success at New Haven for Yale, fashion and the profession turned decisively against him. Like Hitchcock after *The Birds* he never managed to regain that success or preeminent position again. He died, aged 78, from one of the tragic consequences of all of that experimental construction, asbestos-induced cancer.

In the Communist East, meet the modest brutalist, Jadwiga Grabowska-Hawrylak, one of Poland's pioneering female modernists. She came to prominence with her Mezonetowiec (or maisonette

Yale Art and Architecture Building, New Haven, USA.
Architect: Paul Rudolph.

block) at Kołłątaj in Wrocław (1955–58), much in the style of a
scaled down – though still ambitious – Unité, containing 56 two-
storey flats and a parade of shops on the ground floor. And indeed it
was much admired by Le Corbusier. Then there was the Scientists'
House in Grunwaldzki Square (1958–60), which she designed for
researchers from Wrocław University of Technology. This is more of
a classic modernist slab block. Rough, corrugated concrete ran along
the length of the structure – well, it did until renovations smoothed
out the surface – and balconies project from the exterior with mid-
century abandon. Enjoying her work, Grabowska-Hawrylak lived
here, alongside hundreds of fellow residents, for 22 years. But she was
best known for her towering landmarks at Plac Grunwaldzki, a series
of complex and organic concrete high-rises in a district known locally
as 'Manhattan'. More on them later. Born in 1920, she is still going at
time of writing – perhaps proof that her architecture is indeed good
to live in.

Osaka-born Kenzō Tange was the restless brutalist. Like
many of his peers, he combined the urges of an urban designer with
the skill of a hugely creative architect. He was willing to turn the
orthodoxy of modernism on its head, stating that 'only the beautiful
can be functional'. Like the majority of Japanese architects, he
used concrete not in a rough, primitive way, like the Europeans or
Americans, but took great pride in the crisp finish, the smooth shell,
the perfection of the shuttering marks. He would go on to design
some of the most varied and moving structures of the atomic age,
from the studied stillness of Hiroshima Peace Garden (1949–55) to
the almost Le Corbusian monumentality of the Imabari City Hall
Complex (1957–59). There is the smooth perfection of his Kagawa
Prefectural Government Office too (1954–58), whose regular, paper-
thin frame and calm surface detailing is kept unpolluted behind a
tranquil moat. Cobbles and boulders beneath add a further element

of mannered historical Japanese styling. These cool motifs contrast startlingly with the volcanic energy and thrusting gusto of another of his major projects, St Mary's Cathedral, Tokyo (1960–64). Here the bell tower is a startling spike, a lightning bolt striking the ground beside the cathedral. Concrete is draped like fabric across the cross-shaped structure of the church itself, and light cascades into the vast space through strips of stained glass like streams of lava. Perhaps most extravagant and expressive of all was his Yamanashi Press and Broadcasting Centre in Kofu (1962–66). This massive, sturdy, power station-like structure is formed of 16 cylindrical towers, with voids in the centre intended to be filled in and added to as advances and changes dictated. The resulting building is an extravagant absurdity, like battling robots trapped forever in a deadly embrace. Even so, there is a spirituality to his work, a sense of building and individual in harmony. Another long-lived practitioner, Tange died aged 91.

Ieoh Ming Pei, more often known as IM Pei, is still going strong at the time of writing, aged 100 (what is it with these architects and long life?). He was born in Canton and then studied and established his career in the US. Interviewed in the *Guardian* in 2010 he remarked 'It is good to learn from the ancients, I'm a bit of an ancient myself. They had a lot of time to think about architecture and landscape. Today, we rush everything, but architecture is slow, and the landscapes it sits in even slower. It needs the time our political systems won't allow.' His calm, measured philosophy saw fruition in a great deal of monumental architecture, much of it brutalist in approach. His National Centre for Atmospheric Research (NCAR) in Boulder, Colorado (1961–67) is like an abstract group sculpture of figures peering and hunched, curious and hiding. The Everson Museum of Art in Syracuse (1961–68) is if anything even more of a monumental presence, with great blank, cantilevered cuboids suspended and crowded together, spectacular spiral concrete stairs and coffered ceilings of rough concrete. There is both strange movement and calmness to his work, as if familiar shapes have been caught in transition and calcified over millennia. It's easy to feel overawed by these grand forms, with the weight of history and ideas all around.

German architect Gottfried Böhm, the expressionist brutalist, is also still around, aged 97, at time of writing. His Pilgrimage Church, Neviges (1963–68) is one of the world's most famous works of modern placemaking, where undulating forms snake up a slope to the foot of a massive crystalline church, made of rough concrete and perched on the hilltop. This is a concrete version of Superman's Fortress of Solitude, an expressionist jewel that also sits within the brutalist canon for its collision of rough-hewn construction and in-your-face artistic daring. This is a building meant to impress and dwarf the individual, just as religious architecture has for thousands of years. Much as modern figurative art would not have been possible without the invention of photography, this is architecture seen through the gaze of the great modern artists – the cubists, futurists, expressionists and post-impressionists – and translated into concrete.

We have hundreds of architects to thank for the strange and varied brutalist legacy we have been left. For all the lazy talk of the sterility and blankness of modernism, the thing that links these buildings, and these architects, is strength of character. Anybody who thinks brutalism offers mere functionalism needs to stand and take in the personality of IM Pei's vast buildings, rising from the landscape, or Oscar Niemeyer's languid curves. These structures are every bit as awkward, bloody-minded and outrageous as the people who dreamed them up. And in some cases, as long-lived, too.

7.

<u>The</u> <u>World of</u> <u>Brutalism:</u>

Magical Features and Where to Find Them

B rutalism is a truly international architectural movement – you could spend a lot of money globetrotting to try to catch sight of every notable example. Local variants – Metabolism in Japan, Carioca in Brazil – expand the reach and vernacular of brutalism across cultures too. Like the jet engine, steel reinforced concrete is a modern technology that has been embraced everywhere. Just as we can look up anywhere in the world and see contrails from planes, we can also catch glimpses of rough concrete structures on our travels, if rather less often. Brutalism has proved exceptionally useful as a tool of progress. In some countries it has been an aid to post-war reconstruction, in others a central pillar in the creation of entire new towns and cities.

Some cities are stuffed full of brutalist buildings, created in the white heat of that post-war moment. Chandigarh, an entire city planned by Le Corbusier, and Brasília, Niemeyer's great project (with Lúcio Costa) stand as extraordinary examples, so strange they seem almost like proof of alien landings in our recent past. We will revisit them later. And there are the rebuilds of old settlements too – Boston, say, or Glasgow – where the interruptive use of concrete is a big talking point. But while most conurbations will have some rough-hewn monoliths in evidence, they are not as ubiquitous as you might think. Even so, you can find examples in the most surprising of places. And that's often the thrill of appreciating any form of architecture – discovering and then exploring a remarkable edifice you didn't even know was there. So let me invite you onto my private jet, and we'll take a quick tour of some of the places you really must visit.

We land first at Belfast to check out one of the great modern

Palace of Assembly, Chandigarh, India.

Architect: Le Corbusier.

buildings of Northern Ireland. Some of the most interesting brutalist projects have been museums and galleries, and one of the best is the Ulster Museum extension (1962–71) by Francis Pym, his only major project. The exterior is covered with Tetris-like cubist extrusions, giving an uncompromisingly modernist feel to the otherwise neoclassical façade of the museum – I think it complements it rather beautifully, but others have disagreed. This project wasn't a happy experience for Pym, who found all of the subsequent controversy around the building rather draining. He resigned before the project was finished, didn't attend the opening, and subsequently became an Anglican priest.

Never mind, time to get back on the plane. We're off to Lyon now. Unlike the reticent cool of the International Style, brutalism loves showing off. And because of this extravagant attitude, it often makes for excitingly designed stadiums and assembly halls. Take the Auditorium Maurice Ravel, Lyon (1972–75), designed by Charles Delfante and Henri Pottier, for example. This scallop-shaped concrete structure is certainly one of the most eye-catching landmarks in this high-rise modernist district. There is something of the landed spaceship about the auditorium – imagine *The Day the Earth Stood Still* but without the robot. Well used and much loved, it is the centre of the arts for a whole community.

Now it's a short hop on our plane to Holland, to take in the Aula at Delft University of Technology (1959–66). This contains a large auditorium and four lecture halls and was designed by celebrated Rotterdam firm Van den Broek & Bakema. The majestic cantilevered structure thoroughly embraces the absurdist possibilities of brutalism, and rises like a ship in dry dock from the campus landscape. In fact, students the world over are familiar with raw concrete architecture, enthusiastically commissioned by universities and colleges, both old and new.

Even showier is religious brutalism, and there's loads of
that about. Come on, we'll get off the plane at Berlin to visit Kaiser
Wilhelm Memorial Church (1959–63). A strange hybrid, this,
being a kind of concrete rocket set beside the ruined remains of the
old bombed tower – sci-fi meets fantasy. This post-war concrete
structure, shadowing the older ruin, was designed by Egon Eiermann.
Its walls are perforated with intense blue stained glass designed by
Gabriel Loire. The resulting hybrid is like a nurse guiding a patient,
or a child supporting its aged parent. Now if we make a quick hop
across to Switzerland, we can see a rather more straightforwardly raw
construction, the Holy Cross Church in Chur, (1967–69). Designed
by Walter Förderer, it's as extravagant a series of forms as you could
wish to see. This church combines the deep seriousness of a fortress
with the playful polygonal interlocking shapes of a molecule diagram.
The wood-shuttered concrete throughout and the extensive use of
wood on the inside, together with the curious spaces these polygons
create, makes for a spectacular cave system rather than a conventional
church interior. This ability to create unique voids and volumes is one
of the greatest attributes of brutalism, and has resulted in a legacy
of fearless icons of abstraction. Traditional glass box modernism,
meanwhile, was rather more constrained by the search for the perfect
symmetrical curtain wall, the 'floatiest' tower, or the 'glossiest' podium.
In brutalism sometimes even *finding* the windows can be a challenge.
Don't get lost now!

Now one more short flight, over to Milan. Here you will
find another of those concrete university buildings, the Istituto
Marchiondi, in a handsome Chandigarh-style design by Vittoriano
Vigano. The external structural frame sits away from the main walls of
the college, like a crate holding the interior within its protective grid.
Within two years of its completion the concrete had stained badly,
and as you can see, it has fallen into disrepair. The glass is broken,

graffiti marks the walls, and there's litter everywhere. Not much learning going on now, that's for sure. But at least a protection order has been placed on the building, so it can eventually be restored. No, you can't take bits of it home. Empty that bag at once!

Despite the ruin we have just seen, there is a solidity and permanence to a lot of massed concrete that makes it eminently suitable for the creation of government and official buildings. We're off to one of the most famous brutalist edifices now, the former Ministry of Highways building (1973–75) in Tbilisi, the capital of Georgia. Designed by George Chakhava and Zurab Jalaghania, this mesmerizing structure is an awesome engineering feat, stacking long horizontal units on top of each other at right angles, to form voids and projections. It's a classic International Style office block, deconstructed and shuffled before your eyes by someone with the powers of Magneto from the X-Men. This leaves a large vertical three-dimensional grid – 'hashtag brutalism' at its purest. It has been beautifully restored and is now an essential on any brutalist tour worth its salt.

Many sports stadiums favoured rough concrete too. Take the Vilnius Palace of Concerts and Sports (1965–71) in Lithuania, by Eduardas Chlomauskas. This crashing wave of a building was constructed on the site of a former cemetery, and has played host to everything from basketball championships to pop concerts and political rallies. It's now in a parlous state, graffiti-covered and abandoned, but there are at least plans to renovate it.

Come on, back to the plane, we need to get to Macedonia. We're here to see the Post Office in Skopje (1974–89) with its rabbit's ear projections and toy fort playfulness. It doesn't look much now but back in the day, oh yes. Designed by Alvar Aalto protégé Janko Konstantinov, it certainly provided more fun than your average post office, especially with Borko Lazeski's cubist murals on the inside.

That's until it was gutted by fire in January 2013, rumour has it just days after the insurance had run out. Lazeki's irreplaceable murals were lost, and with them a positive representation of Macedonia's turbulent Soviet-Bloc past. Come on, cheer up. We still have more to see.

We're going for a long-haul flight this time, to the University of São Paulo, where pretty much everything is fascinating. The Faculty of Architecture and Urbanism (1961–69) by João Vilanova Artigas and Carlos Cascaldi is a good example of large-scale planning. Here a heavyweight rough concrete box pins down a smaller lightweight glass one, like an unfair wrestling match between International Style and Brutalist. Light, twisted concrete columns hold up this hefty brute, their delicate origami appearance at odds with the uncompromisingly massive structure above. Inside is a social space full of movement and charm. Students are visible around you on every level, from this perspective seen as alien beings participating in a peculiarly civilized arcade game. The surprising lightness, openness and free flow comes from the decision to link each of the six floors with a system of continuous ramps. You should have brought your skateboard.

And now a trip north, to the Salk Institute in California (1959–65). This cunning Louis Kahn confection is a formal avenue of six-storey blocks, mirroring each other across the street. They are divided by a rill, whose continuing flow of water cascades down to fill a pool at one end, taking advantage of the natural steep topography of the site. So far, so Classical. But in the theatrical layout of the buildings, facing off each other as in an old one-horse town, there is also a strange sense of space-age Wild West. If you were to film a futuristic Western, the Salk Institute would make a perfect Mega-City Dodge, don't you think? Regular protruding sections offer shade and shelter, blank windows and balconies overlook the strip. There are plenty of places for cowdroids to tether their hover-horses and fire their laser pistols in deadly duels. What a great Ray Harryhausen movie that would be, *Clash of the Titans* meets *Gunfight at the O. K. Corral*. No? Well, suit yourself.

We're off to Nairobi now. The Kenyatta International Conference Centre (1967–73) is a bit of a wonder. Designed by local architect David Mutiso and Karl Henrik Nøstvik, from Denmark, it's formed of three parts – a faceted, circular 28-storey tower in rough concrete; a rather less dramatic podium section, added to give extra space for World Bank meetings; and the assembly hall itself, the largest conference centre in East Africa, which nestles underground beneath a broad conical roof. This arrangement of parts is another trick of brutalist landscape design – placing large geometric forms in relation to each other to make a unified asymmetric statement. Mutiso calls his assembly hall a traditional African hut and the tower a phallic symbol. Fair enough. Left to run down for decades, the building is finally beginning to be looked after once more.

Back on board for a couple of hours or so, and in Lusaka there's the University of Zambia (1965–70). Designed by South African Julian Elliott, this challenging project was conceived the year after Zambia gained independence and was a great symbol of the new country. Elliott employs the fashionable ideas of the day: the multilevel decks of a megastructure, hosting the many different functions, from faculties to student housing. The result is surprisingly calm when compared to other post-war megastructures, such as the central area of Cumbernauld, a new town in Scotland made notorious by this outrageous piece of overreaching. The massive blank concrete facades and interlocking cuboids at the University of Zambia impart a sense of unity to this enormous project, and its lush green setting and generous outside space helps to soften Elliott's uncompromising architectural vision. Parks and gardens, lakes and landscaping are as much a part of brutalist design as the raw concrete used in their construction. So many of these buildings are in landscapes that are home to fish, coots and ducks, trees, shrubs and grasses – as well, of course, to people.

Let's pop over to India – well, actually, it's a bit of a hike. Achyut Kanvinde's Indian Institute of Technology at Kanpur (1959–66) combines a leggy concrete frame fleshed out with sturdy brick to create a series of exaggerated colonnades beside water. Not conventional brutalism, it's true, but quite brilliant. Kanvinde embraces one of the most celebrated forms of the era, the top-heavy reverse ziggurat. This massed, regular design helps shade staff and students from the sun. (A similar device at the Guildhall School of Music & Drama, in London's Barbican, provides shelter from the rain.) Kanvinde studied under Walter Gropius, whose teaching seems to underpin the work of many of the brutalist generation. It's certainly a rather formal setting for education – the building is a heavy reminder not to muck about.

At Chandigarh, the capital of the Indian states of Haryana and Punjab, there's Le Corbusier's Palace of Assembly (1953–63), another one of those mighty edifices. It is vastly more joyous than many parliament buildings, containing some stunning epic-scale murals in the most vivid colours, alongside fantastical concrete curves, coruscating pools of water and playful cut-throughs in the walls and pillars. The grid collides with something more fluid and rounded – the semi-circular gully of the crown looking like the horns of a gaur, the mighty Indian bison, with the whole edifice laid out like a giant animal skeleton. Here is the expressive nature of brutalism writ large – an artistic, rather than strictly rational, response to site and function.

Back on the plane, and now we're at the Bangladesh National Parliament House, Dhaka (1961–82), designed by Louis Khan. Its long gestation was due in part to the fallout from the violent Bangladesh Liberation War, which halted work in 1971. This modernist citadel has immense geometric cut-throughs in the rough concrete walls, like a logic puzzle left behind by an extinct race of giants, and seems to rise as a mountain over the surrounding flat landscape. Approached via avenues of palm trees and surrounded by water reflecting Khan's mystical symbols the whole building has a strange dream-like quality. What do you mean, you've got jet lag? Wake up, no time for that.

Time for another flight, to Pasay City in the Philippines. Here, on an equally immense scale, is the Cultural Center of the Philippines (1966–81), a grandstanding development, befitting its commissioner, Imelda Marcos, then wife of the Filipino dictator Ferdinand. Its author, Filipino architect Leandro Valencia Locsin, was best known for his cantilevered 'floating' projects, and the Cultural Center, overhanging Manila Bay, is a classic example. Locsin designed the Center, a complex of buildings, in several styles, including brutalist, there's the pristine floating oblong of the Tanghalang Pambansa, or National Theatre; and the Philippine International Convention Center, in a Russian doll formation of smaller shapes being swallowed by larger ones. It's certainly one of the harder to love monuments of post-war architecture – cool if you like Bond villain lairs, I suppose.

Our globetrotting is nearly over – last leg now. Private commissions to design offices gave designers an opportunity to depart from conventional glass box styling. CBC St Leonard's Centre in Sydney (1972) is a crazy power station of a former bank, in the heart of cosmopolitan Crows Nest. It was designed by Geoff Malone of Kerr & Smith, responding to that moment when automation and computerization in banking was first becoming possible. Another one of those reverse ziggurats is wedged up on bloated concrete verticals. Lozenge-shaped and projecting windows break up the massive rough surfaces. It was originally furnished with all of the moulded plastic furniture you could ever wish to see, every bit as playful and fluid as the building itself. I absolutely adore this one, it's quite the Thunderbirds dream. Today it seems a building in denial about how the world has actually turned out, like an amnesiac uncle lost on a high street.

Well that's the end of our tour. You can find your own way home from here, I'm sure.

8.

<u>Sculpture</u>
<u>Club</u>:

The Grey Area Between Art
and Brutalist Architecture

T he Victorians loved a bronze horse and rider or a versifying establishment figure plonked on a plinth. But the 20th century favoured rather different manifestations of public art. Bronzes, yes, but these were more likely in abstract forms. Memorials also, but again these tended towards the universal, the symbolic and the monolithic. Whether it was an office block or a housing estate, art was seen as an essential element, a civilizing influence and an act of generosity. Many of the greatest names in modern sculpture were asked to produce public art. Some of the most striking examples include Barbara Hepworth's *Single Form* at the United Nations Secretariat Building in New York, Henry Moore's *Two Piece Reclining Figure No. 3* at the Brandon Estate in London, and Pablo Picasso's huge unnamed sculpture in Daley Plaza, Chicago. In Britain perhaps the most ubiquitous exponent of municipal post-war art was William Mitchell, a sculptor who worked extensively in concrete. His work is immediately recognizable: usually concrete relief attached as part of a building, in primitive marks and shapes, built up into large-scale decorative pieces, sometimes coloured, often not.

Mitchell built up his portfolio of artworks while acting as design consultant for the London County Council from 1957–65, during which time he produced 49 pieces of art for 27 different sites across the city. His familiar rough-cast concrete art appears throughout Britain in housing estates, shopping centres, office blocks, subways and churches. On Hope Street in Liverpool alone his work adorns two major buildings just metres apart. He provided a strikingly controlled geometric design for the unconventional bell tower of Frederick Gibberd's wigwam-like catholic cathedral, contrasting with the expressive freehand bronze mouldings for the doors. A short distance away, on what is now the Liverpool Media Academy, handmade concrete casts decorate all unglazed surfaces on the ground floor exterior, in a continuous riot of mark making. Arguably this effect is the most successful and familiar expression of his work, with the organic handmade patterns adding a dash of primitivism that subverts the structured grid of modern buildings. My favourite example is outside the old Three Tuns pub in Coventry (now the world's most avant-garde fried-chicken shop), where he used concrete to decorate the walls facing into the Bull Yard shopping precinct with an energetic, free-wheeling Aztec-influenced design. As with much of his best work, it is like the wild, exotic world of a coral reef, packed with detail. You might expect colourful fish to dart from the deep relief work, or the concrete forms themselves begin to sway and pulse.

William Mitchell is not the only artist whose work is associated with brutalist architecture. Pop art sculptor Eduardo Paolozzi was there from the outset, cited heavily in Reyner Banham's 1955 article on the New Brutalism. He also worked with Peter and Alison Smithson on exhibits for an influential art show called *This is Tomorrow*, at the Whitechapel Gallery in 1956. Fittingly, they collaborated on a post-apocalyptic house – half sculpture, half building. The exhibition famously helped inspire, among others, the writer JG Ballard, who later expressed his inner anguish in a succession of futuristic, dystopian stories set in a version of our world immediately recognisable to anyone who had seen these exhibits.

There is a strange tension between the brutalists' fascination with both pop art and primitivism. One celebrates progress and the other harks back to something dredged from our collective past. But there are, of course, some similarities, and they revolve around romanticization. For primitivism it was in misguided notions of the 'noble savage', while pop art had its equivalent in the form of the nuclear family, figures to be both lionized and subverted through the products that defined their lives. Brutalism appeared to see both the primitive and the pop as inspiration.

Paolozzi's creations vary from abstracted figurative sculptures to industrial machine art and colourful geometric murals. Many of his public artworks are exhibited in futuristic environments: *Piscator* is a substantial aluminium-sheen abstracted head, sat outside on London's Euston Station plaza; another, *Head of Invention*, sits outside the former Design Museum building on the south bank of the Thames; and then there are the mosaics designed for the centre of the new town of Redditch. These days many of his public works are under threat: his mural for Tottenham Court Road London Underground station has been partially removed (a third of which was salvaged and is due to be restored and kept at Edinburgh University), and a continuing row over the ownership of *Piscator* has put its future in some doubt.

These pieces are all significant, but the single most famous icon of brutalist art in Britain is the *Apollo Pavilion* at Peterlee new town, created by Victor Pasmore. The artist had been brought onto the new town team to try to add a visual twist to the designs being created by the development corporation's architects and planners. Instead of taking a minor, token role in the proceedings, Pasmore became an integral member of the team, advising on housing design and estate plans. Given this, his artwork for the town is a fittingly large structural piece, rather than a more modest sculpture. The *Apollo Pavilion* is a construction of slender concrete surfaces. It makes an almost-bridge, a concrete playground, a playful, abstract piece of entirely frivolous landscape, all created from the greyest of concrete and the cleanest of lines. It's a generous piece of post-war art, placed within a housing estate and famous worldwide.

Some brutalist buildings are of such advanced modelling that they can be appreciated as works of art in their own right. One such is the Geisel Library (1968–70) at the University of

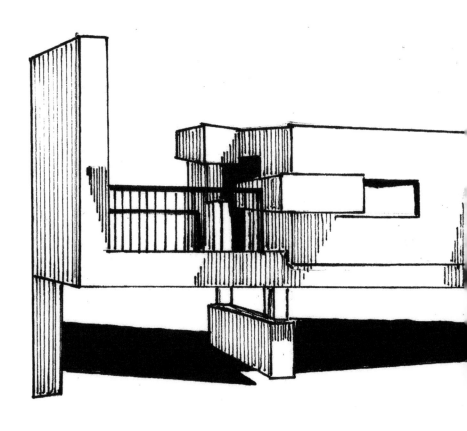

Apollo Pavilion, Peterlee, UK.

Architect: Victor Pasmore.

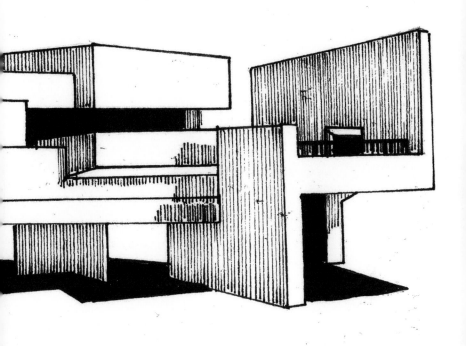

California. Its architect, William Pereira, was already an old hand at creating space-age structures when he came to design this University extension in the mid-1960s. Built on the edge of a small canyon, the eight-storey cantilevered structure stands like a great concrete bloom in bud, a sturdy, spiky succulent rising up in the dry San Diego landscape. The library is named after Theodore Geisel, better known as Dr Seuss, and its eccentric topsy-turvy form makes it the perfect monument to his elliptical rhymes and eccentric illustrations. Books in Nooks? Tomes in Homes? Tracts in Racks? Okay, I'll stop now.

It's not simply high-status buildings such as libraries that express pure artistic intent through their design. The soon-to-be demolished Welbeck Street Car Park (1968–70), behind the Oxford Street branch of Debenhams department store in London, should be a humble, apologetic structure. Instead it's a fascinating patterned grid: a lattice of triangular concrete sections makes up the outer surface of the car park, shapes that act as both load bearing structure and decorative shell. The result is as dazzling as any Op Art painting by Bridget Riley. If even a car park can look this good, why do we put up with so many substandard buildings of significance?

Some brutalist structures are of course created with much higher ambitions in mind. In France, towards the close of the 1960s, there was a desire to produce a National Monument to the Resistance, whose bravery had helped change the course of World War II and whose fight symbolized the plight of the nation. Émile Gilioli, a sculptor who often worked in concrete, created a monument that sits somewhere between sculpture and building – a gigantic stylized hand holding a sun. The Free French Resistance group, the Maquis des Glières, had fought for freedom on the unpromising plateau between the Auges mountains and the Frêtes, where the monument has come to rest. At more than 15 metres (50 feet) tall and weighing 65 tonnes this was the largest commission

Gilioli ever received. Its startling angles, standing out on the expansive mountain plateau, together with the rupture in history it symbolizes, make it one of the most powerful of all artworks constructed from concrete.

The Hiroshima Peace Memorial Park contains other, even more moving, examples of brutalist sculpture. Perhaps the most famous is the Memorial Cenotaph, which like many of the pieces in the park was designed by Kenzō Tange. This saddle-shaped concrete form was unveiled in 1952, the first permanent memorial to the destruction caused by the atomic bomb in the city. The simple mournful shape is there to shelter the souls of the blast and fallout victims. Its cowed form is modest and unassuming, quite the reverse of the Resistance memorial in France, but this meekness and simplicity only adds to the poignancy of the symbol. The city's dust, and all that it symbolizes, has been reborn as the grit in these concrete structures, with both history and tragedy moulded into objects that continue to haunt our imaginations.

9.

The Soul of Brut:

Apartments and Other
Machines for Living In

T he modern apartment is one of the 20th century's most idealized forms. From the functionalist dream of the Frankfurt Kitchen (Margarete Schütte-Lihotzky's simple design for apartments in the 1920s, the precursor to today's fitted kitchens) to the brutal birth of Le Corbusier's Unité d'Habitation, the apartment block has remained an icon of modern ideals: communal, efficient, humane and progressive. It also remains one of the most controversial of all the legacies of modernism. Blocks of flats in housing estates have been blamed for most of society's ills: crime, antisocial behaviour, vandalism, immorality and even fermenting terrorism. They have been deplored as dehumanising environments on the one hand and fêted as the ultimate achievement of modernity on the other. In the post-war period, as architects awoke to the joys of raw concrete, more and more flats came to be constructed in a brutalist style. After all, the examplar, the very instigator of brutalism, had been an apartment block.

The modern flat represents the very soul of brutalism. The most famous buildings might be museums or churches, town halls or libraries, but the creation of mass housing was for many architects what it was all about. In the post-war period local government architecture departments were packed full of modernists, either innovating in the creation of public housing or following the lead of the greats. As with modern art, and the similar motivations found in both pop and primitivism, architects were led by romantic ideas of the 'ordinary' person and how they might live. Empirical evidence and sociological insights were slow in coming; instead, untested patrician visions of new ways of living were imposed on residents, with varied results. But the genuine desire to do the best for the millions of people who were living in overcrowded slum conditions shows an optimism that is lacking in the creation of modern public housing projects today.

Habitat 67, Montreal, Canada.

Architect: Moshe Safdie.

The popularity of the Unité among architects caused imitations of Le Corbusier's masterpiece to spring up across the world. Roehampton and Loughborough Junction in London; Warsaw in Poland; Cleveland, Ohio; Harumi in Tokyo; and Zagreb in Croatia – all these received their homage to the Housing Unit. In Britain, those pioneers Peter and Alison Smithson were influential in a massive development of flats in Sheffield. Park Hill had been a large working-class district of the city, which by the 1950s consisted of dilapidated slum housing. Two young architects, Ivor Smith and Jack Lynn, who had trained under Peter Smithson, took forward ideas propagated by their teacher and his wife. But unlike many of the earlier examples, the flats at Park Hill wouldn't just be a doll's house version of Le Corbusier's. Instead they would take the basic idea of the flats he'd designed, but reconfigure the internal access levels into broad open-air 'streets in the sky'. The rough concrete of Park Hill (1957–61) also feels fitting for the site, where it seems to grow out of the craggy hillside overlooking the city centre. Like the Unité it has a regular 'bottle rack' concrete frame, but instead of that being contained in one neat large geometric block, the Park Hill flats snake along the hilltop like a medieval fort. They form a network of city walls as well as an apartment block.

As in lots of brutalism, such as the Barbican, in London, much of the in-filling between the concrete frame is brick, and in Park Hill the original brick subtly changes in colour as the structure rises. This has been lost in the refurbished sections. Its sprawl, the linked walkways and broad streets in the sky, the moulded balconies and its shop units, all create a wealth of variation in what could have been an oppressively regular design. The landscape itself forced constant adjustments and modifications to the grid, and the architects revelled in the opportunity to produce a more organic form than that suggested by Le Corbusier. The clean lines of the drawings were rendered – not always with great precision – in walls of tactile grey-brown shingle, the use of rough concrete also helping with the organic feel. These days, in a city decimated by industrial decline, the flats are adapting to a new world. Rather than the social housing solution of two generations back, they are now the poster child of urban regeneration, as private flats for young urban professionals.

Le Corbusier's legacy can also be seen in two towering blocks of flats in Britain designed by gruff Hungarian émigré Ernő Goldfinger. The 26-storey Balfron Tower in East London (1965–68) and 31-storey Trellick Tower in West London (1966–74) are massive manifestations of the brutalist apartment block ideal, some of the last of Le Corbusier's legacy to be built. Goldfinger was a difficult man with very strong ideas about what he wanted. To his young staff he seemed to be living out the dreams of an older generation, his peers among the heroic modernists of the 1930s, rather than reacting to new social or political circumstances or design styles. But Goldfinger was convinced that tall blocks of flats, designed and built in a bespoke manner rather than by using the prefabricated kits of the day, were the correct way to go for social housing. The towers and accompanying horizontal blocks he built are like a tableau of muscular figures pumping iron. They are finely sculpted, with the elevators in towers separated from the main buildings, and linked by ladders of walkways. They have a brawny construction, too, from the roughest of brown concrete – like a shingle beach at low tide. And most importantly, they are big, providing hundreds of large flats that were intended for the local councils to rent out. Both towers can be seen from miles away, rising above buildings of much more domestic scale. This initially gave them their fearsome reputations as 'towers of terror', long since surpassed by their appropriations as icons of hipster cool and trendy aspiration. The towers are rather like Goldfinger himself, craggy and uncompromising, offering the unwary a ferociously grumpy silhouette, until you got to know them.

Original residents get misty-eyed reminiscing about their time in these curious landmarks, and many chose to stay, until turfed out by property developers seeking a new, more affluent type of tenant. The views are peerless, and the social cleansing that has gone on in Balfron is a sad example of the purge of working-class residents from good city homes, making way for waves of gentrification.

So far George Finch's Cotton Gardens estate in Kennington (1966–68) has avoided the same fate, although I suspect it is only a matter of time. These three towers, with their irregularly jutting windows and curious upright modelling are quite different from Goldfinger's. Here the flats dispense with the regular 'bottle rack' layout and adopt a more abstract pattern, the very picture of 1960s pop design. The concrete is smooth as plastic, and the blocks are closer to the design of Italian polypropylene furniture than the monolithic regularity of a Le Corbusier.

Rough concrete homes don't have to be high-rise, of course, as another London housing project proves. The Alexandra Road estate in Camden (1968–78), designed by Neave Brown, rebuilds a street beside the busy railway line to Euston as sweeping terraces of concrete and white cement ziggurats. Not since the grand crescents of Bath have such impressive terraced homes been built in Britain. The ziggurats mean that the houses sit back from the central pedestrian pathway, and each home has a garden balcony, whose gentle slope gives none of the vertiginous thrill of, say, a Goldfinger apartment. They are a friendly, happy – and beautiful – manifestation of domestic brutalism, in which hippy openness meets the closeness of a council estate community.

In France, following Le Corbusier's example, there were many experiments on a similar scale. One such is Residence Île Verte, or the Three Towers of Grenoble (1963–67), which when first completed were briefly the tallest inhabited buildings in Europe. These three oval towers, each reaching 33-storeys, were designed by Roger Anger and Pierre Puccinelli. The rough white concrete finish and the clever design of the flats gives a sense of each as a bubble, floating above the world. Each of their small balconies is shielded from the next, helping to create the illusion that each split-level flat has no neighbour. Externally, these complex separations give each block a remarkable hive-like appearance, and their position in a park beside a bend in the river Isère makes them imposing and memorable out-of-town landmarks.

Communist Eastern Europe saw some of the most concerted attempts at creating new flats for workers. Most were system built, but some stand out. One such estate is Plac Grunwaldzki in Wrocław, Poland (1967–75), famous for tower blocks with a curious crocheted appearance to their concrete frames. Known locally as 'Manhattan', the district was rebuilt in the Communist era, but not in the classic 'commieblock' style that had been ubiquitous since Khrushchev's edict in 1957. Instead, the towers were built to a bespoke design by celebrated Polish modernist Jadwiga Grabowska-Hawrylak. Their pale grey and rust-red façades show oval windows (the reason locals cheekily call them the 'toilet-seat buildings') connected by slender vertical strips and alternating short, wide horizontal bands. As a design there are elements of both Art Deco and Art Nouveau to the styling, but the dramatic use of sculptural concrete confirms the towers of Plac Grunwaldzki as quintessentially brutalist landmarks. Admittedly the series of towers look a little worse for wear these days, but Grabowska-Hawrylak still hopes for a renovation in 'noble white' for her project, to make the towers into the gleaming futuristic masterpieces she imagined.

When it comes to a utopian vision of futuristic living, it doesn't get any more exciting than those that came as part of

Montreal's World's Fair – Habitat 67 (1963–67). Designer Moshe Safdie, just 23 years old at the time, had worked up the plans while a student in Quebec. He was as astonished as anyone that they were taken up and built for the expo. These flats are a sophisticated step on from the familiar high-rise and slab blocks that formed most of the brutalist housing projects worldwide. Safdie proposed creating 354 identical flats from prefabricated concrete, but their arrangement was to be deliberately irregular. The resulting structure is a playful work of art, with the units sat on, across and beside others to create a freakily random form. Part Jenga, part ruined city, part Italian hill town upended, the voids and overhangs create a dazzling arrangement. The shapes interlock, and provide walkways and gardens ('For everyone a garden' was one of Safdie's favourite phrases) to give the residents plenty of outside space in their lofty position, high above the Saint Lawrence river. It was the perfect design for an international expo – jaw-droppingly audacious, unlike anything seen before, and ever so slightly bonkers. And, yes, if you were wondering, your instinct is correct: 'Initial models of the project were built using Lego bricks,' confirmed Safdie's company in 2012. Despite its famous concrete finish its author was unconcerned with the material – it was the modular concept that excited him. Although big, the project was in fact intended to be even larger. But what had been envisioned as a cheap prefabricated build turned out to be prohibitively expensive. The residents performed a buy-out in 1985, and the flats have shot up in value over the years – an increase that has to be balanced against the constant bill for repairs on such an experimental structure. Even so, Habitat 67, like so many of these blocks, has proved to be an enduringly successful, inspiring and non-brutalizing place to live.

10.

Civic
Pride:

The Heart of the City, Brutalist Style

odern flats might have been the dream for many architects and citizens, but it's amazing just how many official buildings also use the brutalist style to make an impact too. A trip around any city centre extensively rebuilt in the 1960s and 70s will make you wonder at how unadorned, challenging and sometimes downright crazy brutalism came to dominate midcentury civic architecture. From town halls to arts centres, churches to libraries, brutalism was the widespread choice of mild-seeming civic and religious bodies when commissioning new homes in the post-war period. It appears an unlikely option: grey, bulky, uncompromising and wearing its machine ethics on its sleeve. Yet, for local governments or religious communities wanting to make an impression as daring or forward thinking, it proved a stark contrast to the ornate Victoriana, serious-minded neo-Georgian or plush, playful Art Deco that had been the legacy of previous generations. Instead, this new wave of commissions would in some cases relish the rebellious edge of brutalism, in others retreat behind its massive blank façade. It's no coincidence that town halls and churches were built in the same style as the mass housing schemes that were being constructed around the world. What better way to seem 'one of the people' than to echo the domestic style that was becoming familiar to millions. The ploy had varying results.

Architecture certainly didn't come any more integrated with the local community than it did in the new towns springing up around the world. In Cumbernauld, Scotland, tartan suit-wearing eccentric Geoffrey Copcutt wanted to see if he could design a single megastructure to house everything that you might have found in a traditional town centre: shops, offices, cinemas, hotels, car parks, churches, penthouse flats, libraries and even a dual carriageway. Concrete was the perfect material with which to realize this ever-growing giant, although the tough Scottish climate would demand a particularly hard-wearing structure. That wasn't what it got. Copcutt's vision was never fully realized. This was partly due to poor construction by a company that went bust on the job and didn't leave any plans indicating what they'd done, but it was also due to the architect's intransigence. The sheer difficulty of combining so many different functions within one growing structure didn't help. What remains of the central area today looks rather sad. Seen from afar it's like a surrealist painter's landscape cluttered with awkward composite objects, broken machinery and unidentifiable skeletons.

City halls were rather more achievable. In Communist East Germany architects Rudolf Weißer and Hubert Schiefelbein designed the City Hall of Chemnitz, built between 1968–73. While Weißer was the main architect, it's fair to say that Schiefelbein's work is what made the place so memorable. A decorative façade of geometric concrete tiles covers the entire structure, as if the entire behemoth has been caught in a particularly barnacled net. These days Chemnitz likes to think of itself as the 'City of Modernity', but when the City Hall was built the town went by a different name altogether: Karl-Marx-Stadt. Accordingly, a gigantic statue of Marx by Russian sculptor Lev Kerbel stands beside the building, reminding us of the strange twists of modern history. The City Hall is a wonderful monument to East German ingenuity, and an indication that progressive modernism was far from the preserve of the West.

A rather different Cold War-era city hall can be found in the very epitome of Western power, Boston, USA. In 1962, an architectural competition to find a design had been won by the firm of Kallmann, McKinnell and Knowles. They had approached the challenge through using massed reinforced concrete rather the fashionable glass and steel of the day. The resulting City Hall (1963–68) has the feeling of an ancient classical structure, as a deliberate throwback to the beginnings of democracy and justice. It takes the form of a handsome reverse ziggurat, each floor more expansive than the last. Boxes protrude beneath this, breaking up the monumental façade, all of which is suspended on sturdy concrete pillars. From a distance, the whole building looks like the top portion of a Doric column chopped off, enlarged and pixellated. Kallmann, McKinnell & Knowles also designed a tundra-like public plaza as part of the scheme, an attempt to merge the City Hall with the regular business of the people. The philosophy behind their winning entry was to combine public and private areas, with Kallmann explaining that, 'We distrust and have reacted against an architecture that is absolute, uninvolved and abstract'. Instead they had been attracted by the lure of a heavy concrete structure, as a way of anchoring the modern citizen in something solid and unshakeable. They wanted to produce 'a building that exists strongly and irrevocably, rather than an uncommitted abstract structure that could be any place and, therefore, like modern man – without identity or presence.' Presence it certainly doesn't lack, so much so that over the years this imposing hulk has been controversial, with critics and defenders caught in an ever-escalating series of skirmishes, like Bugs Bunny vs Yosemite Sam. Plans for demolition, which were once far advanced, have been cleverly countered by activists and heritage campaigners, and its future seems assured. Until the next time.

Like city halls, religious buildings have the job of attracting and housing a great number of people. The artistic verve, fearlessness and massive voids of brutalism appealed to the church as well. In Minnesota there's a fine example: Saint John's Abbey Church (1954–61), designed by Marcel Breuer as part of the university campus in Collegeville. The presiding Abbot, Baldwin Dworschak, wanted 'a church which will be truly an architectural monument to the service of God.' Breuer certainly provided that, with his audacious design, requiring tons of 'in situ' reinforced concrete, formed in moulds made

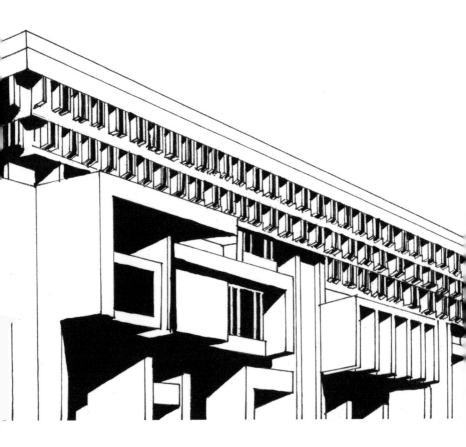

Boston City Hall, Boston, USA.

Architects: Kallmann, McKinnell and Knowles.

by local carpenters. The finished edifice is awe-inspiring, with the bell tower a freestanding sculptural entity, like a sturdy radar dish on legs. Inside, a procession of parabolic arches supporting the roof creates a dramatic series of prosceniums, investing the body of the church with the appearance of a concertina. At one end the concrete has been perforated like a honeycomb, creating the frame for a wall of stained glass.

As we've seen with the Geisel Library, book depositories have also provided golden opportunities for brutalist architects, possibly because their size and the general need to minimize windows makes them suitable for the monumental raw concrete treatment. Take Zalman Aranne Central Library (1968–71), part of the Ben-Gurion University of the Negev in Israel – another outrageous example. Externally and from the side or back it presents a rather inscrutable face to the world, as just a stepped series of concrete walls: impressive, for sure, but anonymous. But from the front or above an entirely different building emerges – one dominated by a cluster of roof lights. They sit on top like bubbles on the surface of dishwater. For the design team, Shulamit Nadler, Michael Nadler, Shmuel Bixon, Moshe Gil and Shimshon Amitai, the library was all about light. Keeping the windows to the top of the structure and channelling the light through galleries and internal spaces makes perfect sense, to avoid light damaging precious books and to allow for the maximum wall space for shelving. Inside the building, the hundred vaulted skylights allow sunlight to filter through to the many different levels and areas of the building. The concrete itself matches the texture of the surrounding Negev desert, while providing a fixed point in this ever-changing landscape, and the appearance of the building could be straight out of Frank Herbert's sci-fi novel *Dune*.

The shadiest brutalist civic structure I can think of is the headquarters of one of the world's most secretive and powerful organizations: the FBI. The J Edgar Hoover Building in Washington DC (1969–75) had been designed back in the early 1960s by Charles F Murphy and Associates, with Stanislaw Z Gladych as the chief architect. It was a tough assignment, because there were many competing ideas of what it should be and how it should be done, and these conflicts created a series of expensive delays. The local authority had wanted a retail arcade as part of the structure but the FBI were, understandably, more keen on security, and thinking bombproof rather than boutique. Occupying an immense corner site, the design is complex, and was compromised from the start by FBI advisors and the General Services Administration – the government department who had commissioned it. The original massive concrete office structure is bested by another, squatter form, which sits above the block and overhangs on two sides, rudely mounting it over the heads of passing pedestrians. An appropriate metaphor perhaps. It was opened in 1975 by Gerald Ford, and contains everything from the labs, morgues and firing ranges you might expect to the printing plant, basketball courts and automobile repair shop you might not.

The J Edgar Hoover building has a citadel-like quality – sturdy and vast, and its rough shuttered concrete and bronze-tinted glass façades so blank as they gaze onto the street. As impregnable-looking as ever, these days everyone wants rid of this great Cold War fortress, its very stodginess seems to summon images of Watergate-era corruption and secrecy, ghosts that still haunt politics today. But this is a building you can love – not for its beauty, and certainly not for the purity of its muddled shape, but instead for its symbolic value. Maybe, in its bold assertion of control, it doesn't represent anything with which slippery modern politicians or FBI agents want to be associated. But its persistence as an unavoidable symbol of justice in the midst of the US capital city is a useful reminder of recent history. It encapsulates those craggy, jowly unelected fixers of the mid-1970s whose faces the concrete seems to conjure in mind, just as clearly as Mount Rushmore does the early presidents. The building is an evasive and unpalatable secret made monumental and uncomfortable. Brutalism as warning.

11.

Cash and Concrete:

The Dizzying Rise
of Corporate Brutalism

Brutalism gives off a whiff of the industrial, even when that's not its primary goal. Why dress up swanky corporate offices as factories? There seems to be a kind of macho myth-making to it, of white-collar worker playing blue collar, living the Bruce Springsteen dream in roughly powerful buildings that act a giant plaid shirt, dressing up pen pushing as factory labour.

If brutalism is as controversial as its critics claim, you'd think it would have been commercial poison. After all, it goes against the norms of contemporary corporate architecture, which tend either towards the anonymous or the self-described 'iconic'. Instead, from factories to high-end offices and shops, the corporate adoption of brutalism as a style was widespread and enthusiastic. Yes, there were instances where the raw lack of cladding often was an accidental solution, forced by cost restraints or expedience. But the ability to create varied, complex and bespoke forms was particularly attractive for the construction of both corporate and industrial commercial sites – from office HQs to factories, hangars, water towers and laboratories.

And so the landmarks of post-war capitalism are often brutalist. Take IM Pei's headquarters for the Overseas Chinese Banking Corporation Centre in downtown Singapore (1975–76). Nicknamed The Calculator, this outlandish monolithic tower looks like a keypad embedded in the centre of a smooth grey pebble. It's a digital Rosetta Stone. The engineer of this and so many other modernist structures, Ove Arup, helped work out how the calculator's buttons – those office floors – could be cantilevered some six metres (around 20 feet) from the smooth concrete surface of the tower. The result is pleasingly eccentric, displaying the requisite wilfulness and ingenuity needed to create any successful hunk of brutalism.

Much as the thought annoys me personally, brutalism might just be the perfect vehicle for freemasons, combining the necessary bombastic effect and cave-like furtiveness: statement architecture that

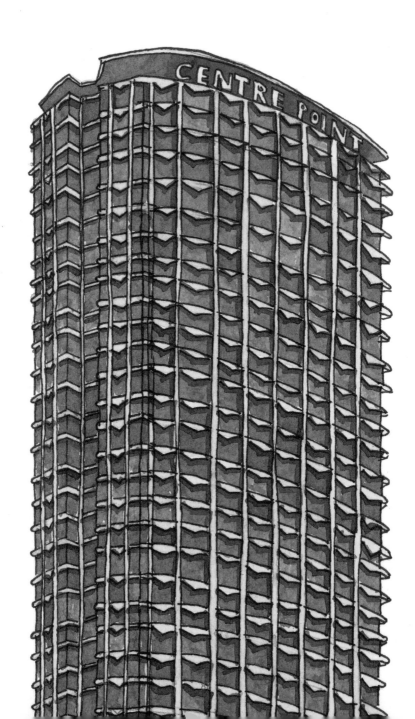

keeps you at arm's length. Sydney Masonic Centre (1973–79) might have been a classic glass box if it hadn't been for the design tricks that play with our ideas of how an office block might function. Designed by Joseland Gilling, this 25-storey office block is immense, and makes you wonder, just what is it they do up there? It takes the traditional tower and podium idea of earlier schemes, but articulates it with such concrete flash and daring that this bastion of covert capitalism also manages to seem a little subversive. The tower is cantilevered above the podium, and stabs into it like God's own pencil, scrawling His name on a secretive deal or two.

Marcel Breuer brought the weight of his ingenuity to a formidable problem: how to combine an office block, a research facility and a warehouse for the Armstrong Rubber Company in New Haven (1968–70). Bring on those trademark precast concrete panels and recessed windows. But that wasn't the most significant decision; his solution for the needs of the business was ingenious. From one end what looks like a simple slab block has actually been split in two, with the tower hovering above the low-rise – a kind of magic trick – the top suspended by two massive piers at the end of the building. The warehouse and research facility occupy the bottom section, with the offices separated into the tower above. It's a visual gag, but of the sort we might expect from post-modern pranksters such as Rem Koolhaas and his holey CCTV Tower in Beijing, rather than a student of the Bauhaus. But still, here it is, a robust 1960s room divider with a hole punched through the middle: the perfect place to display a glass-blown fish, a fat lava pot or some colourfully dyed food.

As with a number of these examples, Centre Point (1963–66), that Central London landmark by the great George Marsh, working

Centre Point, London, UK.
Architect: Richard Seifert.

for Richard Seifert, isn't strictly brutalist. Yes, it is made from faceted concrete panels and has plenty of sculptural dash, but the basic elements of the design – podium, 33-storey tower, fountains and railed walkways – are pure International Style. Yet there's something about the way it evolved in the design stage that made Centre Point edge away from the clean Mies grid of Seifert's earlier tower projects, and towards a more faceted Breuer-type design. The chunky Y-shaped columns that make up the structure create a honeycomb pattern. They stand in heavy relief from the windows, a gesture that creates a much more visually engaging structure than the light glass and steel box that Seifert's team had originally envisaged. Perhaps, then, this is accidental brutalism. It's worth remembering that these were structures created for a pre-digital age. If a company used computers at all, these might be in one almighty block in the basement – a brutalist edifice in their own right. Technology in the mid-60s was just as likely to mean typewriters and adding machines, and computers themselves used punch cards and spools of magnetic tape. With its concrete grid, Centre Point has the look of a scaled-up analogue computer.

Many of the big names in brutalist architecture were drawn to corporate projects; they offered prestige and, perhaps more importantly, a hefty fee. Paul Rudolph produced many, one such example being Endo Pharmacutical Laboratories (1960–64) in Long Island, New York. Like Centre Point, in truth it's not strictly brutalist, combining poured concrete, steel frame and masonry. Unlike the polished surface of Seifert's tower, however, here the concrete is extremely rough. Rudolph had a thing for the muddy impurity of primitive and textural concrete, and rarely opted for a smooth or finely modelled appearance. Here he employs his special 'roping' technique to give a characteristic corduroy surface detail. The finished building is as quirky as they come: a long, low pizza box of a structure, with a basic squareness that's at odds with the many fluid circular forms of its constituent parts. Rows of tubular moldings sit between the windows on the top floor and protrude above the roofline, like streamlined battlements. Triangular, 'Toblerone packet' corridors are narrower at the top than the bottom. Functions jut and protrude from the shell wherever necessary, as if the concrete has leaked and pooled to form ancillary structures. It is certainly the most playful design for a pharmaceutical plant you could imagine – a symphony of cylinders and circles bursting out of a modest low box.

Shopping malls were also good candidates for brutalism. The Tricorn Centre in Portsmouth (1963–66) was one of the most exciting designs of its time. Designed by Rodney Gordon for Owen Luder Associates, the centre was an attempt to provide a new shopping district, flats, pubs, nightclubs and market under cover, with its own car park, in an area on the edge of the town centre surrounded by older shops. Gordon's modelling was bold to the point of delirium, like a geometric toy puzzle rendered in concrete. But it was also a bold statement for the city, in an attempt to create something better than the bland Arndale Centre 'American-style' shopping malls that were springing up across the country. Flaws in construction and maintenance eventually caught up with it and this hopeful, space-age structure was demolished in the early 2000s, leaving its many fans bereft.

12.

Brutal Land- scapes:

Adventures in Town Planning

Alone chunk of brutalism cropping up in a crowded street or isolated rural site is one thing. But for a truly overwhelming experience – epic landscape rather than architectural novelty – let's revisit some of the most forward-thinking places in the world, Chandigarh and Brasília – entire cities of brutalist innovation.

We visited Chandigarh, in passing, on our whirlwind global tour. But how did this symphony of raw concrete and artistic audacity actually come about? India was in the midst of post-independence partition and Lahore, the previous capital of the Indian Punjab, had become part of Pakistan. A new capital for the Punjab was needed and so Chandigarh was founded, situated at the foothills of the Himalayas on flat and fertile land. An original master plan from American architect and planner Mayer and his partner, Nowicki had been developed in 1949, but further plans were discontinued on the death of Nowicki in a plane crash. When Le Corbusier inherited the project, in 1950, he grasped the opportunity to develop a new master plan on a grand scale. And, unlike his city designs of the 1920s, this time the results would actually be built. Here was his chance to show off in the most modern style of the age, one he had pioneered at Marseilles. So many grand and important buildings to create: Punjab and Haryana High Court, the Secretariat Building, the Palace of Assembly, and the university. Being Le Corbusier, he drafted in the most able person he could think of to design them all – himself.

Are there advantages to planning a city all at once, rather than seeing it evolve over centuries? Well, there are the needs and effects of new technology to bear in mind. Take the car, for example. By the mid-20th century, traffic was sending town planners into a tailspin. Road accidents were reaching appalling levels in big cities, and streets were becoming choked with cars. And so, when given the chance to create new towns, planners chose to separate pedestrians from cars as much as possible and to make sure that streets were broad enough to accommodate the predicted traffic. And so in Chandigarh, Le Corbusier planned for the car in building the city around huge roads. Yet the predicted influx of cars was slow to come, and so for years it was largely cyclists who made use of those broad boulevards. Today, as car ownership has boomed in the region, the roads are finally paying off.

In Chandigarh you can see the ghosts of Le Corbusier's earlier plans for Paris. This modern city of government contained pedestrianized sectors, wide highways, parks, lakes and grand structures creating a monumental sense of place at its heart. The architecture is quite something. The Secretariat Building (1953–62) would be imposing enough by itself. It takes on Le Corbusier's irregular grid construction, and expands and exaggerates those sculptural details – extrusions, curves and diagonals – that break the rigidity. From certain points you can see right through it, and at others you can even walk, cycle or drive right through from one side to the other. Purpose built for the serious amount of paperwork being shifted about from floor to floor, a network of long ramps connects the levels of the building. You could get footsore travelling around this place.

We've already explored Le Corbusier's colourful and playful Palace of Assembly (1953–63) on our world tour, in Chapter 7. It is perhaps most notable for the outsize moulded vents and services on the roof, which have been cartooned out of all proportion and break the surface like a whale. Exaggerating the air vents and lift shafts, using them as an excuse to break free of the conventions of polite functionalism and to create decorative forms that are integral to the structure itself, is a classic brutalist ploy. In contrast, there's the High Court (1952–56), presenting a delicate study of lace and arch in raw concrete. Pillars and panels of bright red, blue and yellow sit beneath a sturdy grey umbrella and the complex, deeply shadowed curved shapes are reflected in nearby water. This neat trick makes the heavy structure seem lighter than air, and is one that's repeated in grand architecture all over the city.

Light and shadow is Le Corbusier's game in Chandigarh, just as it had been at Marseilles. Projecting frames and concrete sun-guards keeps direct light off hidden surfaces so that while the sun produces a gleaming white-grey sheen on the rough concrete, shadows create cooler, mysterious spaces for people to walk, work, explore and relax in. Light permeates the buildings in shards and glimpses, both indirect and mysterious. Today, new development surrounds the carefully planned centre, threatening to overwhelm the space and the relationships between buildings. As a place to live it seems popular with the locals, and is notably prosperous and cosmopolitan. With a population of around one million, it's regarded as India's most well-maintained city, and its careful planning has created a rather calm, leisurely way of life.

In South America, Brasília seems at first a much smaller proposition, with over 200,000 people living in the city centre. Yet more than two million have made their home in the surrounding region. The new Brazilian capital city was planned out by Lúcio Costa in 1956, with the work of designing many of the great edifices given to the country's pioneering architect, Oscar Niemeyer. Situated on a high plain, the city is a modernist fantasia. Niemeyer's vision was quite distinct from Le Corbusier's and, in many cases, the buildings in Brasília display more structural daring than those of Chandigarh, and rather less rawness. Take the National Congress (1960–64), with its slender twin towers, linked like a massive capital H. Flanked on one side by the dome of the senate and on the other by the bowl of the lower house, here are simple bold shapes used on a monumental scale:

or two gigantic cereal boxes and a couple of bowls.

In contrast, the Alvorada Palace (1957–8), the president's lakeside home, is a simple long, three-storey box. What could have been a classic International Style grid is enclosed behind the oscilloscope rhythms of the struts that swoop along the façade. They hold the glass box within, like the setting for its delicate jewel. Similar ideas lay behind the structure of the High Court, again a glass box encased behind elegantly faceted pillars. If this were Chandigarh the concrete would be more muscular, the structure heavier, the surface rougher. Instead, Niemeyer's pillars and struts are like the delicate flowing lines of handwriting or, as he saw it, artistic responses to the female body writ large. The National Theatre (1960–66) is a more obviously brutal structure, which from the outside is a truncated concrete pyramid covered in complex square hieroglyphs, with skylights illuminating an indoor garden.

Much of Brasília's centre today is made up of more conventional modern office buildings, making the city a mixture of the truly great and the decidedly average. An odd thing about the centre is its lack of typical Brazilian informal street life, leading to critics to dub this federal capital a giant campus. Authentic street life is instead found in the outskirts – in the satellite towns and favelas where the majority live, where the nation's busy, social streets are recreated and where poverty remains hidden from view of the beauty of the centre.

Many older conurbations have their fair share of brutalist concrete landscapes as well: New Haven and Boston in the United States and São Paulo in Brazil, for example. Historic cities such as Paris or Berlin also contain sizeable post-war districts. In

The Barbican, London, UK.
Architects: Chamberlin, Powell and Bon.

London there are numerous examples of brutalism, but the most concentrated dose is the Barbican (1959–82). This complex of flats, houses, schools, music conservatoire and drama school, underground station, lake, theatres, art galleries, cinemas, hotels and restaurants was masterminded by what we might think of as a resolutely brutalist architectural practice, Chamberlin, Powell and Bon. Not that they would have agreed. An architect I interviewed from the practice called the term 'silly'. The multilevel concrete 'highwalks' take you away from the chaotic ancient sprawl of the city and into a surprisingly calm, enclosed space.

     The joke is that everyone gets lost in the Barbican. So complex is its geography that yellow lines are painted on the walkways, to guide visitors to their destination. As anyone who lives in a city knows, it's easy to get lost anywhere, but perhaps the homogeneity of the Barbican's structure disorients people more than usual. And so it's curious that one of the great criticisms of modernism, by the likes of that charismatic enabler of gentrification, Jane Jacobs, has been that modernism provides an oversimplistic environment for people, one which they grew quickly bored with and rebelled against. Both Brasília and Chandigarh suffered in their early days from a surfeit of space, but this isn't the case with the Barbican's concrete city within a city. It's a great example of how complexity and changes of tone and scale can be used in a cohesive way to create different feelings and environments within a unified whole. I find the Barbican a beautiful protective place, and the only part of the old city where the ancient Roman and medieval walls feel as if they have been extended and their spirit built into the new London. The expensive rough concrete finish imparts a sense of age – of prehistory, almost – to the precinct. Fragments of ruined medieval brick and the reconstructed St Giles Cripplegate Church of 1394 add a startling feeling of ancient ghosts penetrating our modern world. You are surrounded with different textures, rhythms and shapes, a mixture of dark brick and tile, rough pale concrete and smooth white roofing. For me, walking through the public spaces throughout the estate feels welcoming and alive. Being in the Barbican makes me wish more places were like this – well maintained, beautifully thought out, constantly stimulating and yet assuredly themselves. If getting lost were always as interesting as it is in the Barbican, then modern life would be far more pleasurable.

13.

Brutal Bling:

Concrete as a Luxury Item

Perhaps one of the most brutalist moments in modern culture occurred in Chicago, when Motown legend Diana Ross, singing 'I'm Coming Out', ran down the pitch and took a penalty kick, as part of the opening ceremony of the 1994 World Cup. It's hard to think that anyone might have decided to pair a singer well known for her glamorous other-worldliness with the rough and tumble of international football. The choice of song, a gay anthem, was already an incongruous enough choice for a sport so desperate to signal its heterosexuality. She sprinted across the pitch, surrounded by dancers, and approached the goal, lined up her shot and – with seeming indifference – tapped the ball, and missed the target. Regardless, the special-effect goal burst open anyway, and Ross ran through it. Still singing, and oblivious to the absurdity of it all.

Why is this moment brutalist? Well, in its high-end glamorization of rough physicality it encapsulated something of the strange reality of much brutalist architecture. Brutalism wasn't just about creating the essentials of modern life – blocks of flats, shops, integrated infrastructure. It was also an opportunity to show that industrial amounts of raw concrete could become the perfect backdrop to bling. Both rough and showy, it could be both football *and* Diana Ross. As for missing the goal? I'll leave you to decide whether that was the case for some brutalist experiments.

Brutalism's collision with luxury does have a tendency to tip over into camp on occasion, which is just fine by me. Monumental macho gestures, all zuzhed up with *fabulous* soft furnishings and *to die for* concealed lighting. Certainly there is an absurdity to high-end luxury products that is shared in some of brutalism's more showy excesses. Take the unwearable extremes of couture fashion, for instance, where artifice and outrageousness are embraced, and any thoughts of practicality banished. At this level, luxury isn't about considering the functional; instead it's about playing with expensive materials and forms to create something scarce and extraordinary. The fringes of catwalk culture and the edgelands of modern architecture share a tendency to banish the ordinary in favour of celebrating the artfully beautiful, the awkward, the weird.

In their stylish villas and flats the early modernists had been quick to embrace the counter-intuitive luxury of concrete, modelling it into ocean-liner chic and cocktail shaker curves. But it was only in the post-war era that architects began to see the possibilities for juxtaposing concrete at its most raw with the conventional trappings of wealth, such as restaurants and health clubs, more usually associated with opulent, decorative hotels. Le Corbusier's housing units were a first attempt at exploring that conundrum: in these, the middle class could live in a vertical landscape that also allowed them to tone their body beautiful, eat and drink well, socialize and show off, all against a backdrop of industrial-strength reinforced grit.

It wasn't alone. Take Metabolism, a post-war Japanese architectural movement closely allied to the brutalist approach that favoured megastructures and took natural patterns of growth as an inspiration. As might a fashion designer, these architects drew on cellular organization, roots, branches and organic shapes to inform their abstract designs and turned them into extravagant multifunctional megastructures. The Nakagin Capsule Tower in Tokyo (1970–72), designed by Kisho Kurokawa, is a superb example of a building that is as much high-end conceptual art as it is architecture. Exposed concrete and methods of prefabrication were used in creating a network of flats and offices that grow out of two central stems, with the 140 capsules leading off them as leaves and branches. The design makes concrete look lighter than air, with cute circular windows and dinky suspended capsules – like helium balloons trapped in a tree canopy. There was scope within the design to connect capsules to create larger spaces, and to add more if necessary. Metabolism's 'unfinished' nature was another feature of the style: buildings should be allowed to grow as they needed. But sadly in this case, the hard to maintain experimental tower soon lost its extraordinary 'Diana Ross' celebrity poise. In 2010 the water was cut off, bringing decades of habitation and modernist glamour to an end.

Metabolism is just one of a number of 'couture' architectural schools from around the world to be associated with a brutalist approach. Post-war Spain saw the rise of the Organicism movement that, like Metabolism, sought to introduce organic imagery into the mechanized modernist language. A landmark example, Torres Blancas, designed by Francisco Javier Sáenz de Oiza, was built between 1964–69 in Madrid. The apartments and duplexes in this building form a series of clustered 23-storey circular stems that come together to form the tower. The appearance sits somewhere between a stack of coins of different denominations and the irregular rings of Yucca tree bark. To keep the organic theme flowing, the apartments have oval windows, and white marble dust mixed into the concrete makes the structure gleam luxuriously as it stands over the city. Like so many impressive towers, this petrified tree of a building is now inhabited, in part, by wealthy urban professionals with a fetish for the odd.

The glamorous extremes of brutalism didn't just manifest themselves as exclusive apartments. Rough concrete also made a perfect backdrop to the sophisticated loucheness of a ski resort. In 1959, art collector Sylvie Boissonnas and her geophysicist husband Eric decided that they wanted to construct a new winter holiday spot in the French Alps, at Flaine. No safer pair of hands than Marcel Breuer to create it. What they ended up with was a small town of concrete slab blocks, hidden in the mountains. A series of buildings – hotels, gallery, shops, library and a chapel – create an upmarket brutalist village in this inhospitable snowy landscape. Of these blocks,

Hotel La Flaine, with its sun deck overhanging a precipice, was the most dramatic. As if one of those mini municipal Unités had gone on a skiing trip. Sculptures by Picasso, Dubuffet and Vasarely are permanent and monumental additions to the site. The precast elements feature, of course, Breuer's favourite faceted concrete surfaces and inset windows.

The resort was popular when it opened and modernism was still in vogue. It exuded the same kind of edgy, sexy allure and bluntness as a New Wave film starring Alain Delon or Jean Seberg. Indeed, in 1973, it became the first resort in Europe to generate its own snow. Fancy. But by the 1990s maintenance had become an issue (do you see a pattern emerging?), and the whole resort began a long slide into obsolescence and neglect. But brighter days lie ahead, as refurbishment and a renewed interest in Breuer's work and in brutalism generally have begun to rescue the complex.

So, what's posher than a ski resort? An upmarket marina, of course. One of the most exclusive addresses in the world is Marina City, Chicago. A relatively early scheme, completed between 1959–64, it is dominated by two astonishing 61-storey towers. Their tubular, globular, textured shape resembles the hand grips on some gigantic piece of exercise equipment. Architect Bertrand Goldberg's marina complex on the river's edge has it all: a gym, swimming pool, ice rink and bowling alley, as well as a theatre, shops, restaurants and roof gardens. I imagine there are quite a few couture dresses hidden away in the closets of the apartments as well. And, from the number of views from their gorgeously chic semi-circular balconies available on Instagram, it looks like a lot of Airbnb is going on.

Torres Blancas, Madrid, Spain.
Architect: Francisco Javier Sáenz de Oiza.

14.

<u>Welcome</u> <u>to the</u> <u>Lunar</u> <u>Module:</u>

The Cult of Space-Age Design

Brutalism appeared at a curious moment in history. It was the start of the Cold War, when people were still coming to terms with the fallout of World War II. Economies – from Europe to the USA, Japan to the Soviet Union – began to boom in the 1950s, and reconstruction programmes grew along with them. In 1962, at the height of Cold War superpower tensions, the Berlin Wall was erected as a barrier between the Eastern Bloc and Western Europe: paranoia rendered in concrete. Building programmes, art, technology and consumer goods became Cold War battlegrounds, part of state-funded cultural propaganda on all sides. Brutalism, like the arts of the time, absorbed these prevailing anxieties to produce something startlingly new. These revolutions were made possible not only through responses to events but also by new technology and a spirit of space-age optimism. Advances in science would change all aspects of our lives.

Plastics such as polythene, vinyl and PVC all came into their own in the post-war era, replacing objects that up until then were produced more expensively in metal or wood. The basics of 1960s modernity included detergents, vinyl records, disposable pens and electric cabling, all by-products of the petrochemical industry. Culture itself was changed by such products. The emergence of youth culture had been spurred on by the invention of the transistor in 1947: from that Texas Instruments produced the first transistor radio in 1954, just in time to help popularize skiffle and rock 'n' roll, and give a voice to a new generation.

With the invention of Terylene, the first polyester fibre, and Orlon, the first acrylic thread, both in 1941, manufacturing clothing and furnishings became cheap, fuelling what became a fetish for disposability. And it's in furniture and furnishings that we see the closest companions to brutalism emerge. By the early 1960s the sputnik-legged tables and chairs of the International Style were

slowly replaced by sturdier items. This was helped by the increase in the average size of rooms in many newly built flats and houses, along with a recovery from the shortages of the immediate post-war era. Keeping up with the Joneses provided a 'Cold War' in the domestic sphere, as life became more affordable to many through the relaxation of rules around credit and hire purchase.

In Britain, E Gomme of High Wycombe began to produce G-Plan furniture in 1953, as a mass-market version of the bulky design classics of the age. In their monumental teak forms you can see pleasing echoes of rough concrete towers and slabs. Meanwhile, ceramics had moved from the fine moulds of the 1950s to altogether heftier, more textured versions of the 60s and 70s. This was exemplified by the rise of what we now call 'fat lava', a style of pottery popular in West Germany. Its expressive shapes and thick, primitive glazes mimic the experiments in concrete surfaces by the major architects of the times.

Behind all this progress lurked the ever-present threat of Cold War annihilation. The military-industrial complex spurred on many of the scientific advances of the 'jet age', with the streamlined design of aircraft copied by everyone from car manufacturers to designers of domestic technology. A parallel and somewhat more benign offshoot of the jet age, the space race, brought an immense optimism at odds with the nuclear arms race. People embraced its ideas of modular construction and capsule living, with new fabrics, foods and computing technology. The promise of a new era of global travel was born, through super-airports the size of towns and airliners as large as tower blocks. And yet there were chilling portents too – the creation of fearsome new weapons capable of destroying whole cities.

Brutalism sits somewhere between forward-thinking visions of technological progress and a harking back to forms of primitivism prevalent in modern art and the relics of the recent world wars.

Whereas the pioneers of the International Style might have taken their cues from the punchy aerodynamics of fighter jets and the glamour of private travel, the brutalists seem to have created a world befitting the paranoia prevalent in the Cold War. The shadow of nuclear bunkers, tanks, aircraft carriers and concrete fortresses hangs over post-war rebuilding. Brutalism arose as an architecture that reflected the hardships of a generation that had lived through World War II. Its architects may have been designing theatres, luxury hotels or town halls, but these buildings were memorials to a fearful time as much as a vision for the future. Brutalism could be seen as modernism for a wearier, warier world – encapsulating both the optimism of the welfare state in an era of peace and the reminder of an anxious, Cold War age.

Pages 108–109:

A 1970s living room.

15.

<u>Lost</u>
<u>Brutes</u>:

Demolition
and the Absence of the Future

Before many of these challenging buildings had time to settle into collective consciousness, they had gone. Buildings whose concrete forms were once so massive and heavy. Whose shadows once fell across neighbouring structures and streets. There were no traces in the grooves in a carpet or the wear on a staircase, to capture the daily routines of those who had once lived or worked in these buildings. It can be hard to picture where once they stood. Today, many exist only in our minds, and in the cultural artefacts – books, films, photography – that are left behind.

It is easy in a book such as this to point the finger elsewhere – maintenance, vandalism, politics… yadda, yadda, yadda. But of course, sometimes brutalist buildings failed simply because they failed. Architects sometimes overreached what was technically possible, and budgets didn't match ambition. The entire Modernist movement, of which brutalism was part, has almost entirely faded too, just as all successive art movements are superseded by the next, often as a reaction. Perhaps modernism fell foul to a backlash that sought to take revenge for every Victorian railway station or terraced house demolished in the cause of progress.

Whenever it comes to discussing the loss of great brutalist work, two names inevitably come up: Owen Luder and Rodney Gordon, British architects who fully embraced the possibilities of raw concrete and created some of the most emblematic superstar structures of the post-war era. A trio of their most magnificent buildings has now gone: Trinity Square in Gateshead (1962–67); the Tricorn Centre in Portsmouth (1963–66); and Derwent Tower in Dunston, Tyne-and-Wear (1968–72).

The Tricorn was the first to go, demolished in 2004. It was a complex that included shops, a market, flats, pubs, clubs and a car park. Its absence left a hole in local landscape and memory, given that the subsequent promises of regeneration turned out to be, at best, a dream. And when a town loses a landmark as memorable as this the stories and myths grow over time. Next to go was Gateshead's Trinity Square, demolished in 2010. This shopping centre topped by a car park was memorably featured in that 1971 thriller, *Get Carter*, where a grisly end is met by future *Coronation Street* actor Bryan Mosley's character Cliff Brumby, thrown off a ramp by Michael Caine. The building itself came to an equally violent end. Homes all over the North East now contain bits of the car park, broken up and scavenged as mementoes like the Berlin Wall. Finally, the last of the three, Derwent Tower, came down in 2012. This was one of the most unusual tower blocks in Britain, a 29-storey brutalist rocket complete with flying buttresses. Built somewhat against the wishes of the architects, who were keen for a lower level housing scheme due to the poor conditions of the site, the finished tower never really stood a chance. Still, it had its moment in pop culture as well: in 1970 it featured in a TV advert for Tudor Crisps, beating *Get Carter* to the screen. Like all three of these buildings, the Dunston Rocket, as it was known, was a complicated structure that became run down through – you guessed it – lack of maintenance. Result: three irreplaceable buildings gone.

Were the architects to blame? With Derwent Tower, perhaps, in creating a building where they had little faith it could work on the given site. But Trinity Square and the Tricorn Centre were great buildings, wilfully vandalized by their owners' lack of pride in them. I imagine ghosts of the residents of the Dunstan Rocket still pacing the sky where their flats had once stood. If you look carefully shadows from disco dancers at the Tricorn can still be glimpsed from the corner of your eye. And shoppers from Trinity Square will forever be holding up that polyester dress or taking a drag from a cigarette on the edge of the car park.

One of the saddest and most senseless losses was John Madin's Birmingham Central Library (1969–74). The city has become expert at demolishing libraries. The neoclassical version from 1862 was damaged by fire, and its Renaissance-style replacement, opened in 1882, was knocked down, the books and archives moved to Madin's building, which has since been superseded too. The frilly new one, opened in 2013, was de-staffed almost as soon as it was finished due to City Council funding cuts. As with previous demolitions, I feel there was little purpose to the destruction, other than to reflect the restless city's insecurity and damaged self-image.

Madin's library was a reverse ziggurat, broader at the top than at the base, much like the design of Boston City Hall, in the US. As an aside, if you fancy checking out another great example of the form try the State Government Offices in Geelong, Australia (1978–79) by Buchan Laird & Bawden – here's a reverse ziggurat wrapped in concrete ribbon. A gift box.

Birmingham Central Library, with its large internal courtyard to throw light through the reference library wing, was the city's finest brutalist building, and for the prolific Mr Madin perhaps his greatest architectural achievement. Beautifully functional, easy to access and navigate, with plenty of room for the many different collections, it was a joy to browse, read, write and mooch about in. The building had initially been part of a much bigger plan by Madin for a new civic centre to be constructed in a similar style, most of which was not completed. High-level walkways would have linked the new library to institutes for music, drama and sports, as well as shops, offices, a pub, car park and the bus station, creating a modern landscape on a par with the Barbican in London. In an era of global oil crises and industrial action this costly enterprise was abandoned. Birmingham politicians have long sought to make their mark with building projects, and it seems the work of their immediate

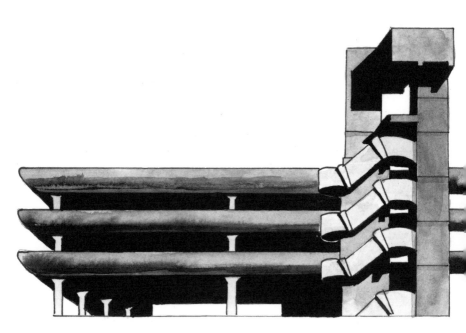

The Tricorn Centre, Portsmouth, UK.

Architects: Owen Luder and Rodney Gordon.

predecessors is always vulnerable to being erased. As machines began to dig into the slender façades and heavy concrete structure in early 2016, pictures of the destruction circulated around the globe, to the dismay of architecture fans worldwide.

Another loss was a bespoke high-rise scheme by Basil Spence in Glasgow, back when Ernő Goldfinger's London blocks were just a doodle on a sketchpad. The Queen Elizabeth Square flats (1958–62) in Hutchensontown in the Gorbals were two tall, slender towers, built in uncompromisingly rough aggregate. Twenty storeys high and housing 200 new homes, they were part of the first wave of post-war redevelopment of Glasgow, replacing the overcrowded and insanitary tenements. Spence's design had all sorts of romantic affectations, including an idea of it looking like a ship in full sail on washday, when all the sheets would be billowing on the stacked verandas. Initially popular with residents, the blocks were never looked after and quickly fell into a state of vandalism and disrepair. The Queenies, as they were known, became early victims of the post-war backlash against brutalism and were demolished in 1993.

The ghosts of these and many other optimistic, grandiose schemes haunt global culture and local memory. Their brief lives have in some cases been catalogued in great detail, and in others left to evaporate. As younger generations encounter their shadows, their lost mass and their dissipated dreams, they'll want answers. What happened to these extraordinary structures, and why? The truth is, people profited from their destruction, whether developers, hungry for new sites and projects, or local politicians and councils, keen to make their mark on the world. So if you love a local brutalist building, record as much information on it as you can, share it online, and keep an eye on it. Changes and demolition occur when those in charge believe, or choose to believe, that nobody cares and that they can get away with it. We can help keep these landmark buildings, and many more like them, viable and well looked after through the 21st century.

16.

Ruined Brutes:

When Rough Concrete
Returns to Nature

There is something about a ruin that sets the pulse racing. It doesn't matter if it's the megalithic remains of a bronze-age burial chamber, a grandiose fragment of Greek Classicism or the spooky cracked shell of a crumbling Victorian villa; the spectacle and narrative of these broken forms intrigue us. Perhaps I've watched too many *Planet of the Apes* films but, for me, it is the landscape of modern catastrophe that holds a particularly potent force. Visions of our contemporary lives and society swept away, the trapping of civilization vanished beneath an earth hungry to reassert itself. Alan Weissman's 2007 book *The World Without Us*, imagining what would happen if humans disappeared from the world, examined the practical details of this ruin: the sewerage systems of cities failing and the contents rising to the surface; the trees and creatures knocking down walls and inhabiting our spaces; weather and natural disasters levelling this unmaintained built environment. It seems that some of the longest-lasting signs of our modern world would be public art: those bronze statues donated to housing estates by benevolent organizations.

In their short lives, some 20th-century buildings have got there already. They've fallen into disrepair or have been utterly abandoned. It's hard to think of a more spectacular example than St Peter's Seminary in Cardross, Scotland (1961–66), designed by renowned Glaswegian practice Gillespie, Kidd & Coia. There are elements reminiscent of Le Corbusier's last major work in Europe, his fearlessly rough La Tourette Monastery in Lyon (1953–57). Both seek to rework the medieval idea of a closed, inward-looking, multifunctional monastery. St Peter's remained a Roman Catholic seminary only briefly, before the falling number of students meant it was suddenly surplus to requirements. Its subsequent use as a rehab unit for drug addicts also ceased decades ago. Now it remains as a baffling monument in the forest, like something left behind by a lost civilization – perhaps a good metaphor for brutalism itself. 'Who was it for?' explorers in this post-apocalyptic landscape might ask, 'and what did they do here?'

Since the late 1980s, when the Church ceased using it, and its abandonment in the 1990s, the beauty of the expensive finishes and the artistry of the architects at St Peter's has been subverted by new types of decoration. Some are the result of graffiti artists, spraying the rough concrete with designs that range from the most basic of tags to extravagant murals, bringing dark and abandoned spaces back to dazzling life. And then there's the imprint of nature, as water, trees, weeds and sun have worked away on the great concrete limbs and ribs. Natural forces are forming a work of land art, somewhere between an Andy Goldsworthy, built from local stone, and a Rachel Whiteread, with the imprint of human habitation, long since departed. And everywhere there's the smell of damp, like a graveyard or underpass.

And it has itself become an art piece. In the summer of 2016 public arts practitioner NVA brought an audio-visual work, *Hinterland*, to the Seminary. This work explored the place as it was when it was built, what it has become and what it might be again. Through music, lights and images echoing around this now curiously organic structure, thousands of people experienced the spaces left abandoned for so long, and took away some concrete memories.

Another spectacular ruin is Miami Marine Stadium, completed in 1963. Designed by Cuban architect Hilario Candela as a venue for sports from boxing to powerboat racing, it was originally notable for its 100 metre (326-foot) long cantilevered roof built from poured concrete. It closed in 1992 in the aftermath of Hurricane Andrew, at which point it took on another life: as a canvas for the city's graffiti artists. It's estimated that 200 layers of paint now decorate the structure, and even the architect loves what the artists have done to it.

But there are smaller ruins too. The remains of Giuseppe Perugini's mind-expanding Casa Sperimentale, or Experimental

House (1968–71) can be found in the coastal town of Fregene, in Italy. The exposed concrete frame is meant to resemble the creeping branches and trunks of the trees that surround it. Red accents, in window frames and railings, are like the autumnal show of Virginia creeper or the seeping oxide from ironstone. Deep recesses and extravagant protrusions give it the most sculptural of forms, a wilfully awkward design that incorporates a series of great, grey concrete circles and dishes on the external walls, sitting in the frame like that most modern of symbols, an egg in a carton. It even has its own drawbridge to isolate the futuristic inhabitants from the outside world, confirming this place as much playground as house. But this Cubist masterpiece is long abandoned. The experiment has seemingly gone awry, the insides bare and weathered, and perhaps the captive aliens escaped. It now has more in common with an artistic folly like Victor Pasmore's Apollo Pavilion in Peterlee.

These structures exist as part of extreme landscapes, and seem on the verge of disintegrating into them. Will Miami Marine Stadium resist the pressure to redevelop this prime site? Might the woods around St Peter's Seminary refuse to relinquish their hold when the developers come to do it up? Has Perugini's tree house 'gone native' and become an organic structure, rather than one we can recognize as a building? Will fragments of all these be dug up by future archaeologists, or their structures re-emerge in the aerial photographs of dogged geophysicists? Or will their ruins become the set of folk horror movies or the place of neopagan rites, whose customs can be traced back to the operation of long defunct smart phone cameras and spray cans? Who knows? The unlit corners, water-penetrated walls, rusting services, weeds and lichen are not going to let on.

17.

Love Lifts Us Up:

The Restoration
of Brutalist Masterpieces

f ruins and ghost stories aren't for you, there are more positive tales to tell. As fashion and culture have changed over the past two decades, many brutalist buildings have found themselves unexpectedly protected, preserved and renovated. Some that were destined for the scrapheap are now listed and treasured, forcing the narrative around them to change. In the UK at least, once listed, local authorities or private developers can't just move in on buildings for an easy kill. Instead, celebrating them has become a duty, or at least a necessity bestowed by official protection. And in some cases this has led to a resurrection for buildings that had fallen into disrepair.

Preston Bus Station, in Lancashire, is one of the more famous recent cases. Keith Ingham and Charles Wilson's design for the influential Building Design Partnership was constructed between 1968–69, and its extravagant monumental moulding could be Brasília rather than Britain. Four storeys of car parking protrude above the bus station, which forms a kind of street-length clamshell of ribbed, upward-curving balustrades. The design concept came not from the architects but from engineers at Ove Arup. With its broad, generous internal spaces, the building feels more like an airport lounge than a bus station. It represents a real attempt at providing the people of Preston with top-quality public building rather than the quiet accidents or bland leftovers we're more used to in today's amenity design. It's currently being renovated.

Property developers Urban Splash are very slowly renovating those gritty streets in the sky at Park Hill estate in Sheffield. Here, council housing at one end of the estate has been made over into a mixture of luxury and lower-cost apartments while the majority of the site remains boarded up. Old graffiti has been rendered in flashy neon, a logo drawn from a cry of heartbreak, and there's talk of a design museum taking up part of the site. It's a strange resurrection, and not one that sits too sympathetically with the building's past.

But then again, one of many copycat schemes, the Hulme Crescents (1964–72) in Manchester, is long since lost, after a gradual descent from dangerously designed family council housing to an adult-only zone, then to art squats and, finally, uninhabited. Demolition followed in 1994. The Crescents contained design and construction flaws that weren't common to Park Hill, and so the Sheffield scheme remains.

One modern British building to have maintained high standards of quality over the years is Denys Lasdun's Royal National Theatre (1967–76), on the South Bank of the Thames. Its continued maintenance and development is probably the difference between commissioning flats for a working class district of Manchester and a national arts centre in central London. Lasdun hated being lumped in with the brutalists but – well, tough luck. His love of sculptural gestures – ziggurats, geometric landscapes, complex splayed towers – meant the kind of bold diagonal or horizontal shapes that were perfect to be rendered in that most plastic and malleable of materials, raw concrete. Like all the most successful architects of the age, he was in a position to get exactly what he wanted from engineers and builders and, also like most, he was an exacting, niggling boss. The National Theatre shows why this fastidious attention to detail was so important, and has resulted in the construction of a truly magnificent building. Everything has been worked through exhaustively, from the kind of stone and aggregate used in the concrete to best reproduce the boardmarks of the wood, through to the lighting – both inside and out – that would best bring these spaces and surfaces to life, creating intimate zones in what could have otherwise been an overwhelming and chilly megastructure.

You can see just how good the National Theatre is when compared to its neighbour, the IBM building (1978–84). Also designed by Lasdun's practice, it was intended to be a complementary building to the theatre. For sure, there are some continuity features

– the long, low concrete balustrades, for example – but on the whole this is a selfish use of the plot and the space. Sloped surfaces at ground level push passersby away from the edge of the building, and the vast outdoor decks overlooking the river remain unused on even the busiest of days. One of the most noticeable differences is that the IBM building is made from prefabricated concrete panels rather than the expensive boardmarked in-situ poured concrete of the theatre. Mimicking such a well-made building in cheaper materials and aping the generous social space with a network of unused private plateaux, the IBM building is an example of how not to extend an idea sympathetically.

Like the Barbican, the National Theatre has undergone a couple of extensive maintenance and adaptation phases since its completion in the mid-1970s. The most recent began in 2013: the NT Future project was taken on by architects Haworth Tompkins, with a brief to ensure it was being used to best of its potential. A new theatre space, the Dorfman, was constructed, as well as a series of workshops in an adjoining building. The front of the theatre was remodelled, with sympathetic new glazing to transform what had been storage areas into cafés and restaurants, and a piazza created on the previously blind north-east corner. Lasdun had high hopes for the long, low horizontal outside terraces he had created on decks above ground as 'happening' new social spaces for the city, but the inaccessibility of these platforms from outside limited this idea. But the new piazza now helps the intimate people-focused interior scheme (part of Lasdun's original design) spill out onto the South Bank at ground level, connecting the building to its riverside setting as never before.

This is the finest piece of extensive restoration and subtle remodelling I have seen on an important brutalist building. The care and attention to detail has brought the National Theatre even closer to its original intentions than the, sometimes compromised,

Royal National Theatre, London, UK.

Architect: Denys Lasdun.

original layout had allowed. Subtle new lighting brings forgotten corners to life. Prints of the original shuttering were taken to ensure that any new construction was as seamless as possible, and the tones of the original soft furnishings were kept throughout. Here is raw concrete at its luxurious, startling, humanized best. The unparalleled entertainment experience in the two main theatres has been enhanced, and it welcomes even more people into its open arms every day. This is a joyous success story, and a blueprint for anyone thinking of starting out on a similar restoration project.

Of course, once restored these places never go back quite to what they were before. Their resurrection brings with it all sorts of contemporary concerns: new cafés at riverside level on the South Bank as well as on the fashionably raised decks of the 1970s; flats in Park Hill restored but attracting a new class of resident. The world spins around its axis, and these renovation projects are not some form of time travel back to how things were, or how they could have been. Rather they project an idea of the past, as interpretive as any of the great Shakespeare productions inside the National Theatre.

18.

<u>Gritty</u> <u>Urban</u> <u>Decay:</u>

How Brutalism
is (Mis)Represented in Culture

I f you only knew brutalism from its representation in culture you might not recognize the actual buildings at all. Perhaps that's why people with no direct connection to it sometimes hate it so much. After all, popular depiction of the style tends to be ham-fisted. Spot a bit of brutalism on TV or in a film, and it's likely to be a dangerous, murky place where crime is rife – a metaphor for failed idealism. If you're lucky it will be the cold, bleak backdrop to middle-class frigidity, similarly signifying some loss of humanity. In fictional media, brutalist flats are inhabited by the untrustworthy and broken, violent criminals ply their violent trade and armed police storm along the balconies, training their sights on council issue doors. In pop videos, a brutalist landscape conveys how urban and 'real' the musician is, how 'down' with the disadvantaged or rebellious kids. Never mind that the architectural backdrop might actually be full of millionaires.

Perhaps the most celebrated representations of brutalism in written culture come in the novels of J G Ballard, particularly the landscape of his 'apocalyptic novels' – *The Atrocity Exhibition*, *Crash*, *Concrete Island* and *High-Rise* – written between 1969 and 1975. I find the first two in particular almost unbearably frightening, more for a sense of the author's tortured state of mind than for the incidents described. *The Atrocity Exhibition* is a series of short hallucinated snapshots of modern spaces – airports, motorways, hotels – filled with glimpses of disturbing events and a sense of impending, incoherent threat, in chapters with provocative titles such as 'Why I Want to Fuck Ronald Reagan' and 'The Assassination of John Fitzgerald Kennedy Considered as a Downhill Motor Race'. *Crash*, which began as one of the fragments in *The Atrocity Exhibition*, takes the drily shocking documentation of car crash injury studies, and recasts them as observations of a new sexual thrill. The overwhelming landscape of cars and their crashes – motorways, car parks and flyovers – becomes erotically charged: flesh is penetrated by wrecked engineering and

bodily fluids are spilled on the tarmac. *Concrete Island* switches the emphasis from car to location, with our fractured hero trapped on a network of reservations beneath a flyover, where a strange primitive society of modern dropouts is forming. Here the concrete landscape is awe-inspiring, like a desert or ocean and just as impassable. *High-Rise* is Ballard's most architecturally 'brutalist' novel. It is set in the first of a new complex of giant self-contained luxury towers, where civilization begins to fail as the services, hierarchies and social order go into terminal decline. The novels are each shocking, bleak, darkly funny and deeply disturbing. These are not the easy sideswipes of a dismissive anti-modernist. Rather they are the fascinated, penetrating gaze of someone genuinely anguished by the possibilities offered by modern society.

After Ballard's shock tactics, mainstream comedy and brutalism might seem particularly unlikely bedfellows, but there are plenty of examples in the TV of the 1970s. Take Bob Newhart, the gentle, urbane American storyteller, whose self-titled proto-*Frasier* psychologist sitcom ran from 1972–78. The title sequence featured the monumental flying saucer futurism of Marina City, and Newhart's character lived in a large International Style slab block, the Thorndale Beach North condominiums. Even more radically, Mary Richards, lead character in *The Mary Tyler Moore Show*, moved into one of the most uncompromisingly brutalist structures in Minneapolis, Ralph Rapson's Riverside Plaza (1967–74). This became her home in the final two series, from 1975–77. Her flat, in the 39-storey McKnight Building – a rough concrete slab block with bright Mondrian-style colour panels within its confidently expressed grid – might not scream 1970s light entertainment, but it's a glimpse into the very different

Trellick Tower, London, UK.
Architect: Ernő Goldfinger.

dreams and aspirations of that cultural moment.

Pop videos have long been a great place to spy brutalism. London's concrete landmarks have been extensively catalogued across pop culture, and in particular the Barbican. In 1965, British pop band Unit 4 + 2 performed their hit 'Concrete and Clay' on its vast construction site, a place continually shut down through industrial disputes. By 1981 it was star of The Specials' clip for 'Ghost Town', with the millionaire pads, galleries and concert halls standing in somewhat incongruously for depressed Coventry. More recent videos for 'Shutdown' by grime artist Skepta (2016) and synth eccentrics Metronomy's 'Months of Sunday' (2015) were shot there too. Meanwhile back in the 1990s, the Britpop wars between Blur and Oasis were played out through Ernő Goldfinger's towers of London. West London's Trellick was somewhat of a recurring motif in the work of Blur, starring in the touristy video for their glorious 1993 single 'For Tomorrow' and name checked in their 1995 ballad 'Best Days'. Balfron, in the East End, cropped up that same year in the bombastic, fiery-tinted film for the Oasis anthem 'Morning Glory'. Catch the walkways and towers of municipal housing estate Thamesmead as the nostalgic backdrop to childhood bad behaviour in The Libertines' 'What Became of the Likely Lads' (2004). Neave Brown's Camden housing scheme Alexandra Road pops up in an experimental virtual reality film for Foals' 'Mountain at My Gates' and in a rather more soap-opera effort for The 1975's single 'Somebody Else'. It's not all about London, of course. I'm particularly fond of Michel Gondry's film for The Chemical Brothers' 'Go', shot in the uncompromising concrete geometries of Front-de-Seine in Paris, a 1970s development designed by Raymond Lopez and Henri Pottier. Part 1930s health and efficiency workout, part beached synchronized swimming routine, the video is an attempt to inhabit the hard landscape with suitably machine-like movement.

In cinema we all know of Stanley Kubrick's appropriation of brutalism as brutalizing landscape in *A Clockwork Orange*. There's the massively blocky lecture centre of Brunel University and the bright perfection of newly built Thamesmead estate. Decades later, TV superhero comedy *Misfits* was filmed on the same estate, the backdrop now run-down and rain-stained rather than a dazzling sci-fi playground. Filmmakers frequently exploit the gritty nature of concrete as a backdrop to action and violence. Hard-hitting 1970s cop show *The Sweeney* loved a bit of concrete. A good example was a 1975 episode, 'Thou Shalt Not Kill!', a bank heist that was actually filmed at Brunel University's students union precinct (Richard Sheppard, Robson & Partners), then a landscape of low concrete parapets and rough panelling. In Antonioni's 1975 film *The Passenger*, Jack Nicholson's tough guy journalist finds himself adrift in the Brunswick Centre in London. Goldfinger's Balfron Tower crops up yet again in not-quite-zombie horror *28 Days Later*, and *Blitz*, a violent 2011 vehicle for gruff tough-guy Jason Statham.

Whether representing our rough recent past or our bleak urban future, brutalism seems a perfect visual shorthand. When London's newly completed South Bank Centre stood in for a 26th-century prison planet in the 1973 *Doctor Who* serial 'Frontier in Space', nobody was in the least surprised. This was a landscape of space-age grit, after all.

But, as we have seen, brutalism doesn't always denote urban toughness. These edifices are often the everyday manifestation of government or corporations, and so become the perfect settings for tales of high-level political intrigue. The Watergate complex (1962–71) in Washington DC was the essential location for Alan Pakula's 1976 film of *All The President's Men*, given Nixon's clumsy attempts to have the Democratic offices there bugged. The slick, curved Italian design of the complex conjures up the era every bit as much as Robert Redford's flares or Nixon's surly TV denials. Time and again, classic American conspiracy thrillers from the 1970s show the brutalist headquarters of government and business as the blank faces of surveillance, corruption and threat. Modern takes on the genre continue the theme: in 2014 the stylish BBC TV spy series *The Game* attempted to recapture some of the Cold War era's slippery spirit, effectively using the abandoned shell of Birmingham Central Library to stand in for the MI5 office of the day.

Perhaps the most curious brutalist location in film is an imaginary one: the winter fortress in *Inception*, Christopher Nolan's 2010 sci-fi thriller. It plays with ideas of 'dream architecture' – be that the map of a dream and the structures within that, or as a metaphor for storytelling and the creation of imaginary worlds. In the movie the daring heist team dive into the subconscious of their victim in order to plant an idea. The architecture of the dream they create has to be complex, like a maze, so that they can fool the dreamer by pulling them deeper and deeper into the game. Different layers of dreams have different architecture: first is the early 20th-century city, with its sturdy bridges and blocks; then there's a Mies-ian shiny mid-century hotel; beyond that we're into a concrete hospital fortress. One of the most striking things about this fortress is its similarity to William Pereira's Geisel Library in San Diego, a sculptural extravagance that is the very opposite to the mindless monotony so often associated with modernity in filmmakers' minds. As an imaginative representation in a film so obsessed with architecture, it's one of the most interesting portrayals of brutalism in popular culture.

Yet depictions of post-war architecture usually tend towards the negative, serving as places for social realists and pop commentators to show they're in touch with the dispossessed. In such places, abandoned by civilization, society collapses; instead there are encounters with nightmarish gangs of zombies or droogs.

Luxurious apartments buildings stand in for the bleak sites of inner city depravation, and quiet estates for the haunts of gangland central. Intoxicating as they are, sometimes it's best just to forget these images, wander along and see for yourself.

19.

<u>Covetable</u> <u>Concrete</u>:

The Unlikely Fetishization
of Brutalism

The first time I noticed that post-war architecture – and brutalism in particular – was becoming trendy was on seeing the Trellick Tower depicted on a tea towel, in the mid-noughties. It seemed a ridiculous thing, this cosy household item printed with a rather stylish line illustration of the 'Tower of Terror'. But, as it turned out, it was an inspired move. The designers had seen the emerging fashion for vintage furnishings of the 1950s and had made a connection with the architecture of the time. Festival-of-Britain-style Ercol bentwood chair designs were back in vogue and going for vast amounts on eBay but the buildings of the period were still somewhat frozen out, amid discussions on the merits – or not – of post-war design. In Thatcher's Britain, trapped between the crashing fortunes of the post-war welfare state settlement and a populist derision at all things 'modern', brutalist architecture had been vulnerable to trigger-happy local politicians and landowners, determined to make either a quick buck or a fibreglass or faux brick mark on the landscape. But now brutalism was benefiting from a process of modernist rehabilitation, a trend achieved as much by designers of products, textiles and graphics as it was by writers, campaigners and historians. It's an interesting lesson in the way that culture changes over time, even if the objects around us – ones we might hate one day and then covet the next – do not.

In 2011 I interviewed the designers of that Trellick Tower tea towel, Hannah Dipper and Robin Farquhar of homeware company People Will Always Need Plates, which they founded back in 2003. 'It turns out, a lot of folk love a bit of concrete and are quite astute in their architectural tastes,' said Dipper, remarking that Trellick Tower was by far the most popular image they had produced. It gave them the confidence to pursue their interest and, as she explained, 'Whenever we see a concrete masterpiece that we love, we always try to imagine it as it looked in the mind of the architect when he sat at his drawing board... Or how it looked when brand new and spangly, before 30-plus years of rain and smog destroyed the exterior finishes.'

Alongside Trellick they have illustrated the Alton Estate in Roehampton, Denys Lasdun's Keeling House, Trinity Square in Gateshead and, of course, the Barbican. I asked Hannah what the reaction to their designs had been from people who lived or worked in the places they illustrated: 'Often they seem surprised by our choice, but mostly rather pleased. Many of the owners have purchased ware from us, and we've been lucky enough to get a good nose at some of their homes, in return for a free delivery! Trellick residents are particularly keen to share their memories of growing up there and seem utterly delighted that we love it.'

To some extent this appropriation of post-war architecture has helped fuel the gentrification of formerly working-class districts like the Park Hill flats in Sheffield or Denys Lasdun's Keeling House in East London, a rundown masterpiece of social housing that famously sold for £1 to canny developers in 1999. More recently, 'Mid-century modern' fairs, vintage shops and online small business platforms such as Etsy have fed an appetite for the post-war optimism of modern design to middle-class consumers, keen to bring some space-age glamour to interiors made beige, bare and bland by a decade of advice from TV property experts.

Today you can buy brutalist maps, badges, Christmas cards, cushions, fabric, illustrations, tote bags, T-shirts, magazines, postcards, mugs, tea towels, plates and bus-pass wallets, in a frenzy of merchandising that rivals the Moomins or Disney's *Frozen*. Now that it's a popular topic, there are entire sections on brutalism in many bookshops. A rash of books – yes, well spotted, including this one – have celebrated the buildings that once outraged a generation. There is black and white photography to emphasize the monumental forms and rough textures, and colour to bring a more nostalgic, observational edge. There are books to make cut-out models of paper engineered slab blocks alongside historical treatises, lighthearted travelogues, biographies and monographs. Meanwhile, the buildings themselves are being gentrified, reclad, neglected or demolished, their fate beyond the control of the individual consumer, who can look after a mug of Brasília's cathedral or a card of Alexandra Road in the snow but, sadly, cannot stop the destruction of Durham University's beautiful Dunelm House or the social cleansing of Park Hill. A more practical measure might be joining organisations such as the Twentieth Century Society, who campaign to protect them.

I suspect there are now more brutalist fans than there are brutalist homes. For most, a pillowcase of Boston City Hall or a paper model of Kaliningrad's House of Soviets has to suffice. But brutalism seen through a lens – be it books, photos, products or social media – is no substitute for experiencing the real thing. The mass, the volume, your place in all that space, and the touch, smell and sound of a building – all these will live with you afterwards in indefinable ways. Just as seeing the sun at a certain level in the sky might remind you of the start of the school term or the inevitable end of summer, so the echoes of shoes on a concrete floor or the shadows on a staircase from a skylight can take you right back to moments in places you have known and loved.

20.

Emotional Concrete:

How Does Brutalism
Make You Feel Today?

Brutalism is a shock to the system: a rush of blood, a broken nose and a sore head. Despite the earnest philosophizing of Le Corbusier, the Smithsons and Reyner Banham, when seeing a brutalist edifice for the first time one's response is entirely irrational. What *is* it? Why does it look like *that*? And *how on earth* is it doing that? Sometimes when encountering a brutalist building I sense those shock waves still reverberating, as they have for decades.

Often I give up trying to rationalize my feelings. Why are so many post-war churches quite so thrillingly odd? Perhaps because, well, they just are. They are great art, and like a lot of great art, you might understand all of the theory in the world, but ultimately something beyond that affects you. You might instinctively understand something of it, or be completely speechless with awe. Perhaps you'd reject it. You might even pass by the same building for years without a second thought until something, or someone, causes you to look at it in a different way. Suddenly you notice that there was an idea there all along; all it took was for you to engage with it.

One of the things I love about brutalism – for me, the *very best* thing – is its absurdity. The lunacy of apartment blocks posing as factories, or offices as industrial plant. It makes me happy to see the great lumbering shaggy dog of Wyndham Court (Lyons Israel Ellis, 1966–69), for example, visible as the train pulls into Southampton. There it stands, its elevator tower 'ears' up, and lanky front legs hopping over a low wall, staring indifferently at the trains going by. The variety of brutalism is intoxicating: the ghost of the simple Unité was soon shrugged off and forms became more and more extraordinary: the playful disco Cubism of the Sirius building in Sydney; the teetering stack of coins that forms the Torres Blancas; the seemingly randomly plonked domino boxes of Habitat 67. Town halls could be deconstructed classical monuments turned on their heads or car batteries the size of entire city blocks; government offices become giant hashtags in the sky; office towers impersonated enormous calculators. The combination of reinforced concrete and open minds liberated a generation of architects. It let them off the leash to play.

In the past five years or so the fashion for brutalism has reached some sort of high tide, but high tides recede. What will be left when this tide goes out? Fewer landmarks, that's for sure. And some that are changed beyond recognition. But it's not just the buildings we have to consider, of course: most importantly, it's the people. Lives have been changed and enhanced by this reversal of brutalism's fortune. Residents and workers can suddenly feel more proud of 'their' brutalist buildings. Young people have encountered something extraordinary and often ignored. And others have been persuaded to love a bit of raw concrete, to admire the sculptural daring of a group of ventilation shafts or some oddly shaped windows. And even though this tide of popularity for brutalism may go out, perhaps it won't retreat so far, and more people will be ready when it comes back in again.

It's not been an entirely positive story, of course. The Grenfell Tower fire has certainly made more people aware of the plight of those in post-war social housing, and made residents in similar blocks feel more vulnerable too. Ultimately all this talk of style and design is irrelevant if the buildings we live and work in are unsafe, underfunded or left unmanaged. Safe, decent architecture of any style is a basic that we should expect. To compromise those structures through careless remodelling or cutting corners can have catastrophic effects. The lessons from this monumental tragedy should inform further decisions on the future of all our buildings, regardless of age.

It brings back that old Reyner Banham conundrum to me. Is brutalism an ethic, based on the kind of lives we dream we used to live, rooted in experience and hope? Or is it an aesthetic, conveying an expression of artistic purity that we can never quite live up to? Well perhaps, after all, it has to be both: deeply rooted in human history and experience, while also reflecting the ideals of a better life back at us.

Around the world campaigns have been launched to save great structures that are slipping out of our reach: the glorious stepped, modular flats of the Sirius building on the bank of Sydney harbour and the secretive, sociable students' union building, Dunelm House, beside the River Wear at Durham University, for example. Generations of people have genuinely loved such places, in ways that aren't some exercise in posturing or rebellion. Developers or university administrators might regard brutalist buildings as weird concrete monstrosities, standing in the way of the future. But to those who love the buildings, they are a part of history – not just of great design, but of life and humanity.

I love brutalism for its usefulness – *Homes*! *Hospitals*! *Universities*! – as much as for its art-for-arts-sake swagger – *Sculpture*! *Air vents*! *Asymmetry*! And it's in the synthesis of both that brutalism comes into its own. In his utopian novel of neo-medievalism, *News from Nowhere*, William Morris imagines modern society destroyed, and replaced through socialist revolution by an arts-and-crafts-based return to the land. But with brutalism the revolution isn't imagined – it actually happened. The sweeping improvement in living conditions for many was brought about through post-war housing schemes and welfare state support systems, and went much further towards creating that utopian ideal than Morris and his revolution ever did. His movement resulted in prettier houses for the middle classes in garden cities and private estates, but didn't really touch the wider issues created by the industrial revolution for the slum-dwelling working class.

Brutalism was both housing revolution *and* industrial revolution. It was innovative apartment blocks, schools and health centres as well as factories, offices, power stations and hydroelectric dams. Post-war modernism, of which brutalism was, after all, just a part, was a project interrupted by larger forces, from which it has since rowed back. It was not perfect, and it did not solve all our problems, but in it we can glimpse a heroic attempt to improve all our lives.

Brutalism was a concentrated burst of that desire to build a better world, with extraordinary structures that exceeded their remit of mere function. It ran aground on the global financial crises of the 1970s and the conservative backlash that reverted to Victorian models of philanthropy and private enterprise. As brutalist icons are either left to crumble or are reinvented for a curious present, we should look beyond the superficial and remember the intentions of the best of the architects, planners, builders and engineers of the day. Today, brutalism preserves the memory of an inspired municipal moment – optimism captured in amber. Because, wilful and outrageous as it was, there is heart beneath that raw concrete shell.

Index

Further Reading:

Reyner Banham, *The New Brutalism*, Architectural Press, 1966

Leonardo Benevolo, *History of Modern Architecture: Volume 2, The Modern Movement*, Routledge, 1971

Barnabas Calder, *Raw Concrete*, Heinemann, 2016

Peter Chadwick, *This Brutal World*, Phaidon, 2016

Le Corbusier, *Towards a New Architecture*, Dover [reprint], 1927

Lionel Esher, *A Broken Wave*, Pelican, 1983

Adrian Forty, *Concrete and Culture*, Reaktion, 2012

Marcel Gautherot and Kenneth Frampton, *Building Brasília*, Thames and Hudson, 2010

Miles Glendinning and Stefan Muthesius, *Tower Block*, Yale University Press, 1994

Rebuilding Scotland edited by Miles Glendinning, Tuckwell Press, 1997

John Gold, *The Practice of Modernism*, Routledge, 2007

Elain Harwood and Alan Powers (ed), *The Sixties*, The Twentieth Century Society, 2002

Elain Harwood and Alan Powers (ed), *The Seventies*, The

Twentieth Century Society, 2012

Elain Harwood and Alan Powers (ed) *Housing the Twentieth Century Nation*, The Twentieth Century Society, 2008

Elain Harwood, *Space, Hope and Brutalism*, Yale Universty Press, 2015

Elain Harwood and James O Davies, *England's Post-War Listed Buildings*, Batsford, 2015

Owen Hatherley, *Militant Modernism*, Zero Books, 2009

Owen Hatherley, *Landscapes of Communism*, Allen Lane, 2015

Charles Jencks and Karl Kropf (ed), *Theories and Manifestoes of Contemporary Architecture*, Wiley, Second Edition, 2008

Zhongjie Lin, *Kenzō Tange and the Metabolist Movement*, Routledge, 2010

Oliver Marriott, *The Property Boom*, Pan Piper, 1969

Douglas Murphy, *The Architecture of Failure*, Zero Books, 2012

Stefi Orazi, *Modernist Estates*, Frances Lincoln, 2015

Alison and Peter Smithson, *The Charged Void*, Monacelli Press, 2001

Nigel Warburton, *Ernő Goldfinger: The Life of an Architect*, Routledge, 2004

Websites:
archigram.westminster.ac.uk
ballardian.com
c20society.org.uk
dirtymodernscoundrel.com
docomomo.com
fuckyeahbrutalism.tumblr.com
instagram.com/the_brutal_artist
lccmunicipal.com
modernist-society.org
municipaldreams.wordpress.com
nastybrutalistandshort.blogspot.co.uk
somethingconcreteandmodern.co.uk
sosbrutalism.org
team10online.org
therubbleclub.com
thisbrutalhouse.com

First published in the United Kingdom in 2018 by
Batsford
43 Great Ormond Street
London WC1N 3HZ

An imprint of Pavilion Books Company Ltd.

Volume copyright © Batsford, 2018
Text © John Grindrod, 2018
Illustrations © The Brutal Artist, 2018

ISBN: 9781849944427

A CIP catalogue record for this book is available
from the British Library.

10 9 8 7 6 5 4 3 2 1

Reproduction by Mission, Hong Kong
Printed and bound by Toppan Leefung Printing Ltd, China

This book can be ordered direct from the publisher
at the website:
www.pavilionbooks.com, or try your local bookshop.